A Comprehensive Guide to Starting Forex Trading

Masaf I. Rahman

Funny helpful tips:

Maintain a feedback loop with stakeholders; their insights are valuable.

Set aside funds for emergencies; unexpected expenses can arise in business.

A Comprehensive Guide to Starting Forex Trading : Master the Art of Forex Trading: A Complete Beginner's Handbook for Financial Success

Life advices:

Stay informed about industry trends; being ahead of the curve gives a competitive edge.

Mix up your workouts; varying exercises prevent plateaus and keep the training engaging.

Introduction

Step into the world of forex trading with this illuminating beginner's guide that lays the foundation for a rewarding journey into the complex realm of foreign exchange markets.

Begin by unraveling the essence of forex trading itself. Understand the dynamics of currency pairs, the concept of spread, the significance of pips, and the intricacies of lot size. Dive into the empowering realm of leverage, distinguishing between long and short positions, as well as the ever-present bull and bear markets.

Navigate the crucial process of opening a trading account, demystifying the role of brokers and comprehending their indispensable functions. Explore the powerful MetaTrader 4 (MT4) platform, available on desktop and mobile devices, that serves as a trader's essential toolkit.

Master the art of placing orders effectively with insights into different order types. Delve into the world of charts and indicators, exploring trendlines, level lines, and channels that illuminate market trends. Uncover the potential of various indicators that aid in accurate decision-making.

Embark on a deeper exploration into trading systems, ranging from parallel trendlines to Andrews' Pitchfork. Learn to craft a comprehensive trading plan and delve into the intricacies of supply and demand trading, demystifying the reasons behind levels' effectiveness.

Peek into the dynamic interplay between bears and bulls, understanding the strength of levels and the nuances of filled and unfilled orders. Grasp a nuanced understanding of candle types, where the approach you take matters.

Discover the value of different time frames in trading decisions and explore the elusive concept of the trading zone. Delve into the essential aspect of risk management, calculating risk/reward ratios, determining stop loss, and target profit.

Equip yourself with the importance of maintaining a trading journal to track your progress, identify patterns, and enhance your decision-making. Immerse yourself in practical examples such as the analysis of USDCAD on February 10, 2016, and AUDUSD from April 27, 2016, to June 07, 2016, to comprehend real-world application.

Address the critical topic of drawdown and risk tolerance, understanding how much to risk while safeguarding your trading endeavors.

Concluding with a thoughtful reflection, this guide encapsulates the essence of forex trading for beginners, imparting invaluable knowledge and perspectives to initiate your journey toward becoming a proficient forex trader.

Contents

CHAPTER 1: FOREX TRADING

Basics and nomenclature

What is forex trading?

The forex (foreign exchange) market is where currencies are traded. The concept of currency trading was around long before the term "forex" was coined. Almost any person, at some point in their life, has had to go to a bank or foreign exchange broker to exchange currency. Currency exchange is important, and it impacts our daily lives whether we realize it or not. The necessity for exchanging currency is perhaps the main reason for making forex the largest and most liquid market in the world.

Prior to making the forex available to retail traders (that is, regular people like you and me), currency exchange was only available by walking into a bank or broker with your physical money in hand. Forex trading was the realm of big financial institutions, central banks and hedge funds (these are what I call "big players"). Nowadays, however, you can trade currencies electronically on your own computer. The transactions happen between traders all over the world, on a 24-hour basis, five days of the week. Being traded in almost all major financial centers around the world is what allows for such flexibility. Actually, the 24-hour possibility was one of the main reasons I got involved with forex and left the stock market. With a 9-to-5 job, I realized that the forex is the perfect option for my lifestyle. Although you are able to trade currencies, it does not mean that your orders go directly to the same pool as those big players' orders.

I will expand on this important concept later in the book in the section dedicated to forex brokers.

Before diving into further details, I will list the common currencies that are tradable across the forex market, the corresponding symbols, and some common phrases in forex trading.

Currency pairs

USD: US dollar. This is the most influential currency in the forex market.

EUR: Euro. The European Union currency is the second most important currency.

GBP: British pound. "Cable" is the common name among forex traders for the exchange rate between GBP and USD.

CAD: Canadian dollar. You will sometimes hear it called the "Loonie", the popular name for this currency.

AUD: Australian dollar. It is commonly called "Aussie" among traders.

NZD: New Zealand dollar. This is commonly referred to as "Kiwi" among traders.

JPY: Japanese yen.

CHF: Swiss franc.

What does this information mean for currency trading? It is essential to understand that currencies are traded in an exchange format. That means you always buy or sell a currency in exchange for another currency. I know this is intuitive, but in comparison with the stock market, it can get confusing. In the stock market, each symbol represents a single company and you do not need to buy or sell another stock in exchange. Currencies, however, are traded in pairs, such as EURUSD, AUDUSD, NZDCAD, etc. The first symbol (on the left) is the main currency that you trade in exchange for the second currency (on the right). When you buy EURUSD, by definition you are selling USD to buy EUR. Likewise, when you sell EURUSD, you are buying USD in exchange for EUR.

Another important factor is the concept of *major* and *cross* pairs. There are seven major currency pairs in the forex market that have USD on one side: EURUSD, USDJPY, GBPUSD, USDCAD, AUDUSD, NZDUSD, USDCHF. These are the most frequently traded pairs, and many traders do not trade anything besides these. As might be expected, the other currency pairs that do not have USD on either side are commonly called cross currency pairs or crosses. The most actively traded ones include EURGBP, EURCHF, EURCAD, EURAUD, EURNZD, EURJPY, GBPJPY, CADJPY, AUDJPY, NZDJPY, GBPCAD, GBPAUD. The main difference between these two categories of pairs is the liquidity and hence, the spread.

Spread

Similar to any other financial market, the forex market has spread. It is simply the difference in the price of buying and selling a currency pair. The more liquid the pair, the lower the spread. Low spread is one of the main reasons many traders trade only major pairs. In most cases, the spreads are not constant, and they change based on the time of day and the liquidity in the market. Due to the advent of online forex trading and computer-based transactions, the spreads in forex are only a fraction of what you will see in a physical bank or exchange broker board. I will explain more in the next paragraph, where I talk about "pip".

Pip

The unit of measurement, or the smallest number to represent the change in the value of the exchange rate for a pair, is called a "pip". In practice, a pip is the last decimal point of a currency pair exchange rate. In most cases, the currency pairs are displayed down to four or five decimal points. The fourth decimal point is considered as the pip value. For instance, if USDCAD moves from 1.2132 to 1.2133, you would say the USD rises by one pip. The exceptions to this are the JPY pairs, which are displayed to only two decimal places, and the second decimal point defines the pip. An example of the spread in pips and the lot size is shown in Figure 1. I'll discuss lot size a little later in this book.

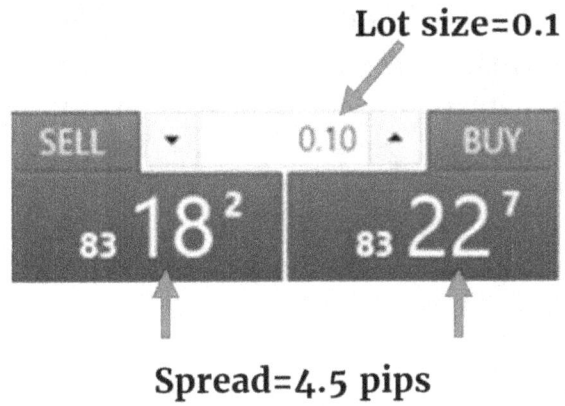

Figure 1. Spread and lot size

In many cases, traders report their profit and loss in terms of pips, rather than in an actual dollar amount. That is because the dollar amount is a function of the number of pips, lot size and leverage. I will go over the latter two in the following sections.

Lot size

Historically, forex pairs were traded only in specific amounts called lots, which are the number of currency pair units being traded. The standard lot size is 100,000 units of a currency pair. Nowadays, there are smaller fractions of a lot known as mini (10,000), micro (1,000) and nano (100) lots. As you can imagine, the change in the value of a pair measured by pip is a very small percentage of the pair value. Hence, to take advantage of this small change, you need a large number of unit pairs to gain any significant profit.

For instance, the value of a pip when trading one standard lot of USDJPY at 113.50 will be (0.01/113.50×100,000), which is equal to about $8.80 per pip according to the following formula:

pip value = 1 pip × lot size/exchange rate

The exchange rate in this formula refers to the rate of exchange from the second currency (JPY in this example) to your account currency. In this example, the account currency happens to be USD, but if EUR is the account currency, the EURJPY rate must be used as the exchange rate.

The big question is how you as an individual trader can afford to trade one standard lot. That comes next.

Leverage

As seen above, trading standard or even mini lots requires a large amount of money. This is done through the leverage that your broker offers to you as a loan. In most cases, your broker takes a $500 to $1,000 deposit and will lend you a buying or selling power of $100,000, which is a 100:1 leverage on a $1,000 deposit. Of course, the loss or gain from any trade will be applied to the cash balance in your account. So, if your trade is going against you up to a total of perhaps 80% of your cash balance, your broker will close your trades in order to protect you and themselves from losing more that 80% of your cash. This is what is called a margin call in the world of trading. You do not ever want to be anywhere near that amount in any of your trades.

Long and short, bull and bear

Similar to stock market trading, you either buy or sell a currency pair. In this context, buying a pair is equal to being "long" on that pair. At the same time, you are selling the right side of the currency pair which is going "short" on that currency. Let's look at an example: when you buy USDCAD, you are "long" on USD and "short" on CAD. The opposite is true when you sell USDCAD. If you have never traded stocks, keeping this example in mind should help to clarify some of the lingo that is used. However, for someone with a stock trading background, "shorting" a pair could sound odd. I recommend reading online about "shorting" in the stock market should you be interested in learning a little more about it. Likewise, you would call a market or pair "bullish" when it is trending upward. Trending downward is call "bearish".

How to open an account

Rather than going into more detail at this stage about the common language that is used among forex traders, I will explain concepts as I go along.

Let's explore now how to open an account. Opening a forex trading account is fairly straightforward. It requires your personal information, some government-issued ID, bank account information in some cases, and a method of depositing money into your account, which could be a credit card, check or wire transfer, depending on where you are in the world. In the following paragraph I will go over the most standard way of opening an online live account with a broker. In the next section, I will discuss how to choose a broker, and, for the sake of education and simplicity, I will stick with a simple option.

Figure 2 shows a snapshot of the page for a well-known forex broker in North America. As you can see, the process is straightforward.

They will need your personal information and a bank statement as your proof of identity. Upon completing this process, they will take from a few hours to a day to clarify your information. You will be able to deposit a minimum amount ranging from $100 to $1,000 using a credit card, check or wire transfer. You will use your credential to log in to your online or MT4 trading platform. Before diving into the MT4 platform section though, let's discuss a bit more about brokers.

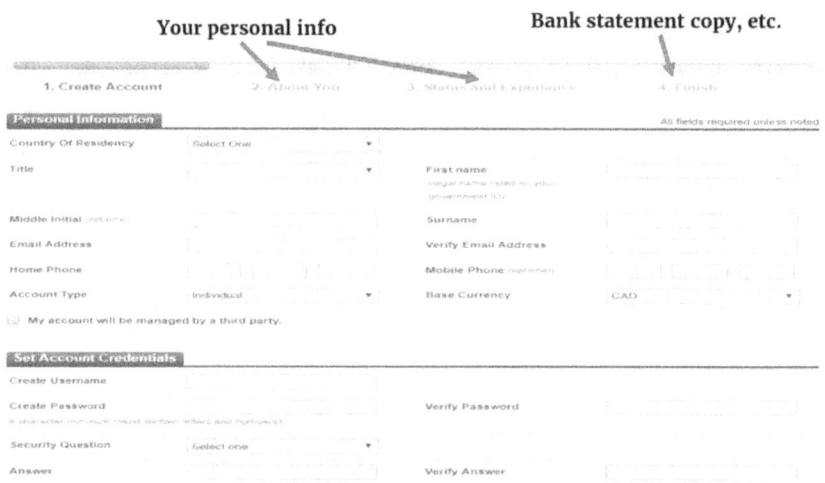

Figure 2. Example of live account setup

Brokers and what they do

I didn't realize how important the role of a forex broker is until I performed a thorough search on that topic. How did I find out that it is important? Like many of you who have been trading for a while, I noticed how smart "Mr. Market" is. He knew exactly where my stop loss was. I will explain more about stop loss orders in the coming sections. For now, it suffices to say that the stop loss is where you place your exit order from a trade in anticipation of the trade going against your expectations. I was amazed at how the market knew exactly what I was thinking. It felt almost as if the market was waiting for my orders and then seemed to turn against me as soon as I placed them. I know for a fact that I am not alone in feeling this way. After reading and learning about the structure of the forex market, I found out my feeling was somewhat right. There is a "smart" mechanism hidden behind the scenes that, as traders say, "shops for my stop loss".

Let me give a brief explanation of the forex market structure and how brokers operate. It is worth mentioning that the knowledge and information I compile here is a fraction of what is available online. Please feel free to search and dig deeper if you are interested. For the purpose of this book, the following paragraphs should be sufficient.

For over five decades, major currencies have been exchanged in a free market format where the supply and demand determines the rates. This free type of market has allowed the currencies to fluctuate against each other more frequently than before. In return, it has provided for the concept of speculation on future exchange rates. The big banks' thorough knowledge of the forex market has enabled them to acquire large profits from such speculations. However, large volumes of transactions by these banks have caused shortages in liquidity at certain times and resulted in incomplete transactions. The intuitive solution was to increase the number of participants in this market to generate liquidity. This resulted in hedge funds and some retail forex dealers becoming forex market participants, albeit definitely less experienced forex market participants.

The structure of the forex market is an over-the-counter (OTC) format where there is no central exchange similar to the stock exchange. The large transactions that comprise the top ranked percentage of the forex market are made in the interbank market. The interbank market is where all large money centers trade currencies against each other. While accessing such a market seems impossible, platforms such as Electronic Broking Services

(EBS), created by some of the largest banks, have allowed direct access to this market. Other systems were also developed, by Reuters for example, to compete with EBS. Of course, the clients of these systems are still big banks.

The second largest participants are international institutions, which include major national banks, who will exchange local currency into most other global currencies. They offer you a rate that is somewhat different from what the interbank market shows. Some retail brokers, such as electronic communication networks (ECNs), also exist in this category. The third part of the forex market is occupied by the retail forex brokers who deal with the second group. You and I deal with these brokers.

Retail forex brokers provide a service that enables retail traders to speculate about the exchange rate of the interbank market with only a fraction of the money that is required in that market. Prior to this concept, access to the interbank market by someone with, let's say $20,000, was impossible. There are two types of brokers in this category: electronic communication networks (ECNs) and market makers. The ECNs are still exclusive to those traders with larger capital in the scale of $50,000 to $100,000 (referring to the minimum deposit amount required). They provide direct access to the interbank market. On the other hand, market makers display their pricing based on their internal set amounts. They execute orders based on what they publicly display. This price is usually an aggregate of the pricing they receive from a pool of market maker competitors. Unlike market makers, ECNs offer their pricing based on what they receive from the interbank market participants. Another difference is the commission versus spread. ECNs normally charge a fixed commission for any transaction, while market makers make their money from spreads. Let me explain a bit more about the market makers, who are the ones most retail traders deal with.

As mentioned, a market maker is a broker or dealer firm that provides buy and sell pricing for a currency or commodity on a continuous basis (i.e., 24 hours a day and five days a week). Their pricing has to be competitive with the rest of the market makers. The market maker makes the market by providing immediate execution of a buy or sell order at the expense of holding the opposite order in its books. Market makers are often the counter party to their client's order, meaning they open an opposing trade, which is made from their own inventory or by aggregating a net position and placing an offsetting order through their liquidity provider. In short, they will make their money when their client loses money, a practice that is clearly a conflict of interest. However, they offer a free trading platform, reasonable minimum deposit requirements, high leverage and a low spread, all of which are otherwise not available to traders like us.

At the same time, they have the important role of providing liquidity to the market. In contrast to ECNs, market makers do not deal with much risk when the market opinion or "sentiment" of the market participants is neutral. In such situations, they make money on the spreads, since one set of trades is offset by another set of opposing trades. However, when there is a strong imbalance in the opinion of market participants (i.e., when the market is trending), market makers try to make their profit by increasing the spread and/or placing mirroring orders through their liquidity providers. The latter is called hedging against the trending market. This is an important lesson that I had to learn the hard way. All you need to be aware of is that more often than not, there is an incentive for the broker to trade against you. However, this becomes problematic when they deal with clients with large capital, or with scalpers (short-term traders who get in and out of a trade in a matter of seconds or minutes). When all is said and done, we need to acknowledge that without these brokers, we would not be able to profit from the forex market. So, the moral of the story is: do not blame everything on your broker. Just ensure you understand how brokers work and make their money.

To conclude this section, it is worth noting that you can always check whether a broker is regulated. The OTC nature of the forex market does not mean that its participants are not regulated. Perhaps the best-known regulatory bodies in the forex market are the National Futures Association (NFA), the US Commodity Futures Trading Commission (CFTC), the UK-based Prudential Regulation Authority (PRA) and Financial Conduct Authority (FCA), ARIF (Switzerland), ASIC (Australia), CySEC (Cyprus), and SFC (Hong Kong). For instance, you can check the name of a broker in the NFA website to ensure they are regulated. I emphasize that the information here is only a fraction of what you can find by an online search and I encourage you to do so. More knowledge is more power.

MetaTrader 4 (MT4) desktop and mobile platform

Upon the completion of your registration with your broker of choice, you will have an account number and password. The MetaTrader 4 (MT4) platform is the most commonly used free desktop software that is available for download from your broker's website. Although the MT4 setup is well-documented and readily available online, I would still like to go through the basics to ensure we are trading on comparable platforms. If you are familiar with the MT4 setup, or if you're an experienced trader, feel free to skip this section.

Figure 3 shows the four steps (A to D) that you must follow in order to set up a demo or real account on your MT4 desktop platform. Click to "Open an Account" on the file menu. The first step (A) is to look up the name of your broker and scan. Once you find the proper server (demo or real) and your currency of choice when you opened the account, go to the next step. In step (B), you either enter the account number and password for your real account or opt to create a demo account. If you select the latter, step (C) will ask about your personal information and the initial deposit in your account. I recommend not entering a very high and unreasonable value here. The reason is that you want to simulate your real account as much as you can. In the last step (D), a random account number and password will be created for you. I suggest keeping a copy of the information in this window for your future reference.

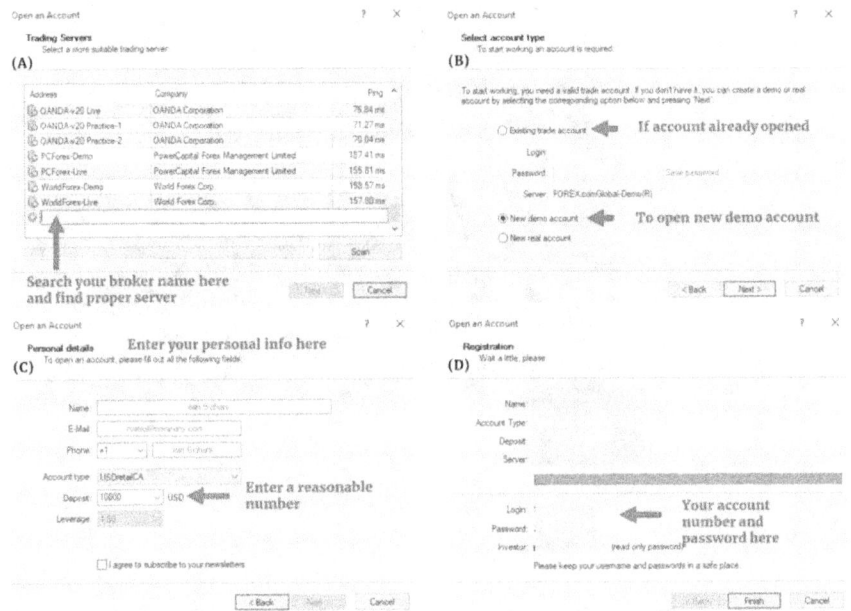

Figure 3. Steps to start a demo or real MT4 account

Once you click on the "Finish" button, you will most likely see a window similar to the one shown in Figure 4.

Figure 4. First look at the MT4 platform

It was this first window that threw a flurry of unknown shapes and figures at me when I looked at it for the first time. If this is the first time you are seeing this, do not bother looking at all of these windows. Simply close as many windows as you can except for the "Terminal" window at the bottom. You will need to open a new currency pair chart using the top left corner button. The chart I use has a much simpler look, similar to the one shown in Figure 5.

Figure 5. Simple chart on the MT4 platform

As you can see, these charts are less terrifying than the original default setting. You can use the annotations in Figure 5 to create a similar-looking chart on your own platform. You can save templates for your future charts and then simply load those templates on any chart you open. The one-click trading button is another useful tool that I have enabled in my settings. Although it's a feature that isn't used very often, I at times have found it helpful.

Before moving to the charting and indicators, let's take a look at the MT4 mobile platform. It is a valuable tool to check on the status of trades and to open and close trades in the case of an emergency. About half of the time, I do find myself trading on my cell phone or tablet.

Look up the MT4 app in your app or play store. Open the application and follow the instructions in Figure 6. The only change I would make is to change the chart setting to "advanced" mode, which will allow you to see the spreads on the list of pairs. Feel free to add and remove your currency pairs of choice in the "pair list" menu.

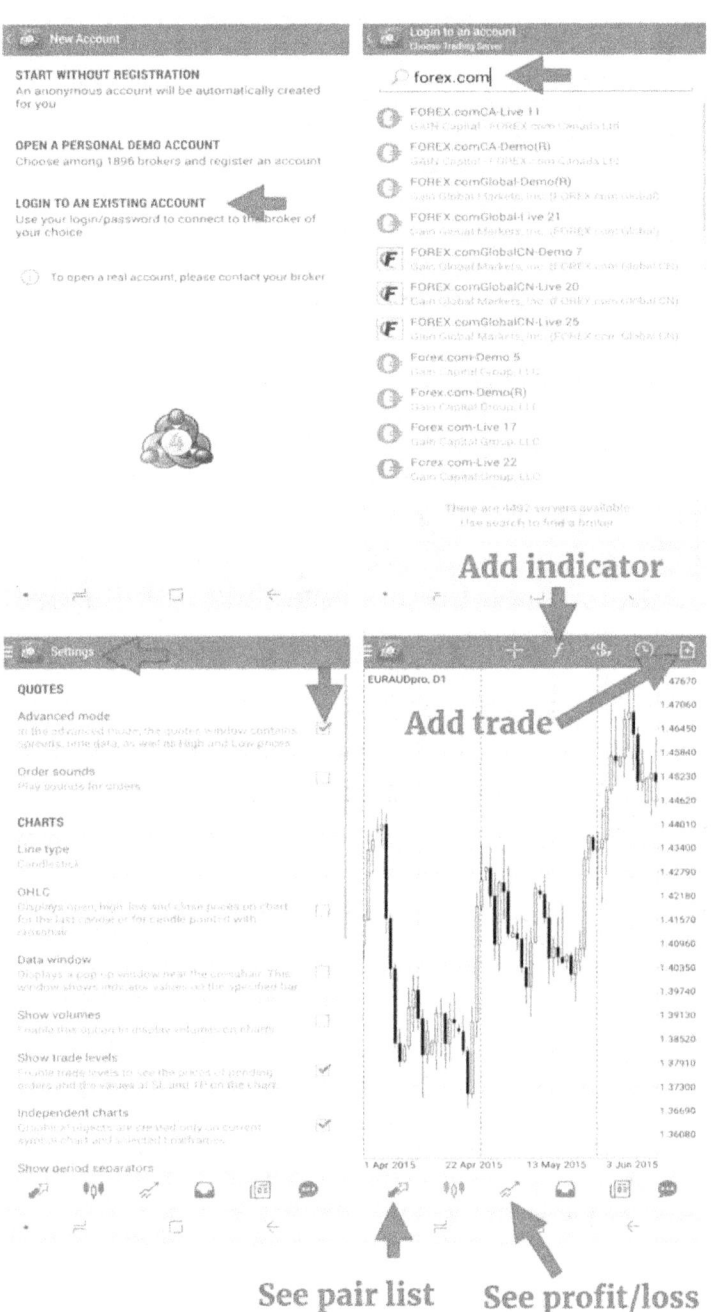

Figure 6. MT4 mobile application

The "Profit and Loss" tab is a useful tab for looking at the overall and individual performance of your trades. You can close or modify your trades by holding your finger on each trade, and that will open a "Modify" window.

Types of orders

It is important to understand the types of orders that can be placed in the forex market. In general, there are two distinct types of orders: market orders and pending orders. The former refers to those orders that are placed at the current price of the market. Pending orders, however, are placed at a figure that is different than the current price in anticipation of a specific price level being reached. Both categories include buy or sell orders. In the following paragraph, I will explain in more detail the subcategories of the pending orders, as the market order is self-explanatory.

The first group of pending orders are called "limit" orders. These refer to those scenarios where you place an order that is different than what the current price is. It will be activated once the price you have chosen is reached. If the order is placed above the current price, it will be a "sell limit" order. You anticipate that the price will drop back down once it has reached that level and therefore you would like to sell at that price. You do not want to sell at a lower price, not even one single pip lower than your limit order. Similarly, the "buy limit" is placed at a price lower than the current market price in anticipation of the market price bouncing back up from that level. Again, the limit order means that you are not willing to pay even one pip higher than your buy limit price. The MT4 platform makes it very simple to place limit orders. Simply right-click at a higher (for sell limit) or lower (for buy limit) price than the current market value and select the Limit Order button (as shown in Figure 7).

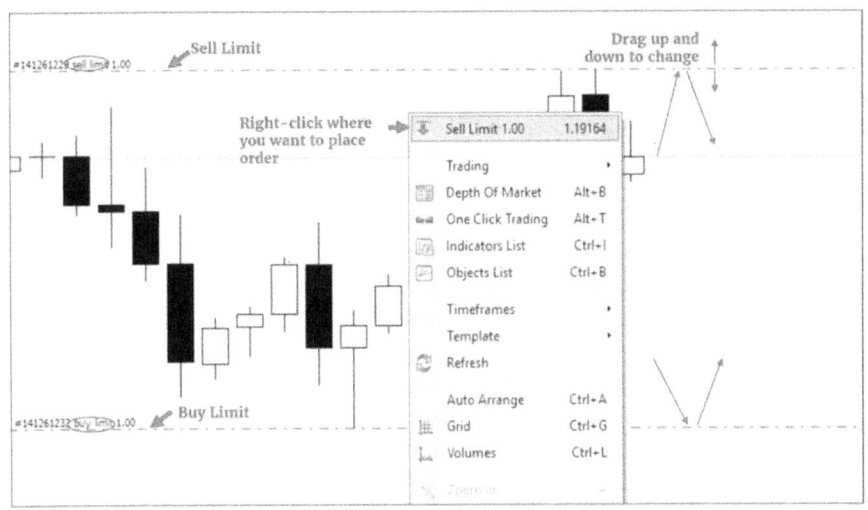

Figure 7. Limit orders on MT4

The arrows on the limit order represent your anticipation of how the price will react when it reaches to those levels. You can also simply drag your order up and down to change the entry price.

The next group of pending orders includes stop orders. A "sell stop" order is placed at a level lower than the current price. A sell stop means that you will not sell until the price drops below a certain level. The "buy stop" acts the opposite way: you are not willing to buy unless the price moves up to a certain level. This type of order is commonly used when trading the "breakout" of a range or channel (both of these terms will be explained in an upcoming section of the book). In order to place a stop order, right-click at a price of interest on the chart and select the appropriate stop order under the Trading tab. Figure 8 illustrates this process.

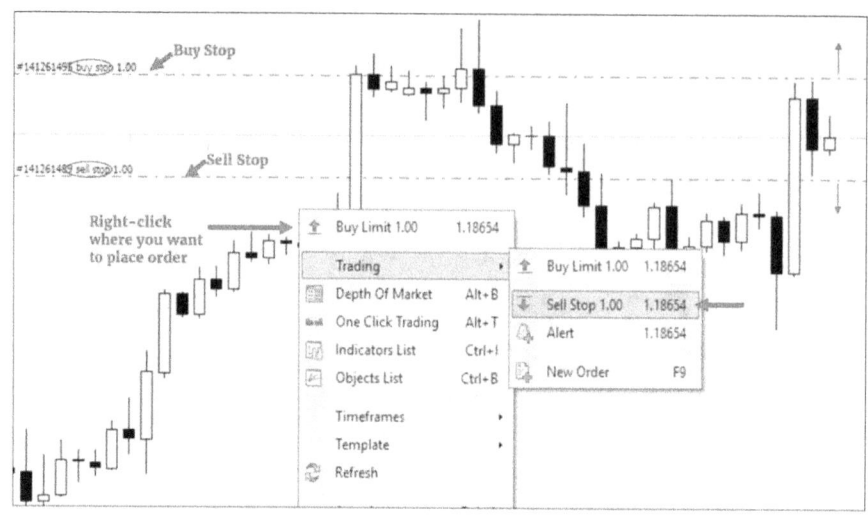

Figure 8. Stop orders on MT4

The last set of orders, and perhaps the most important ones, are the "stop loss", "trailing stop" and "target profit" orders. A stop loss is an order on the opposing side of your trade, which is the opposite of your entry order. This means that if you order a sell, as seen in Figure 9, your stop loss order is somewhere above the entry price. The stop loss is intended to protect you from losing all of your account if the trade does not behave the way you anticipated. As soon as the price reaches the stop loss, your trade will be closed, with a certain amount of loss in your capital that has been pre-determined by you. It is worth noting that the stop loss can be considered as a separate order on its own. For example, the stop loss in the case of Figure 9 below is a "buy stop" order with the exact lot size of your original entry order. This is an intuitive yet very important fact that is often neglected by traders. I have included some more commentary about this simple concept in the following chapters.

The target profit is where you are willing to close the trade with a pre-determined profit. The easiest method to place the stop loss and target profit is to left-click and drag your computer mouse on an already opened order. Going to the opposite side of your trade will place a stop loss order on the chart. Dragging in the same direction as the entry order will place a target profit on the chart.

The third order is the trailing stop order. When a trade moves in the direction you expected, and you have made some profit, you can place this type of order. It is placed at a defined distance from the price in order to protect your profit from being completely wiped out by any sudden movement against your trade. Figure 9 also shows how to place the trailing stop order on the chart.

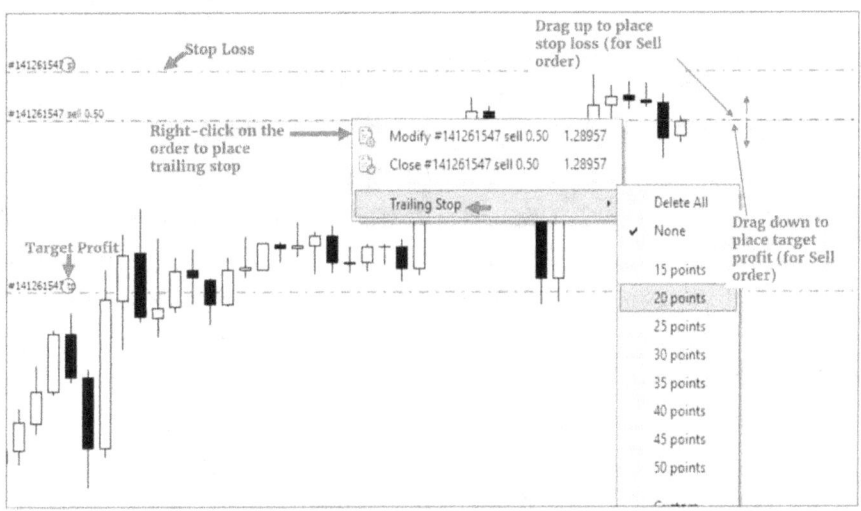

Figure 9. Stop loss, trailing stop and target profit for a sell order on MT4

Charts and indicators

The charts shown in the previous section are the exact charts I use in my daily trading. I use a candlestick chart, but it will not make any difference if you choose the bar chart. A quick overview of the candlestick chart and the information it encompasses is shown in Figure 10 (A). Candlesticks are an abstract way of showing the price in a specific time frame based on the opening, closing, low and high prices. A candlestick has two major components, the body and tails. The body of a candle indicates the distance between the closing and opening price over the time period of that candle. The larger the body, the stronger is the move away from the opening price. A bearish candle indicates the price has dropped while a bullish candle indicates the price has risen.

The tails of a candle, on the other hand, indicate a temporary pressure on the price which was immediately met by a stronger opposing force that rejected this pressure, thus making it only a temporary pressure on the price. An important point that you should consider is the fact that the presence of a long tail has a hidden meaning to it. For the "Long tail" example shown on the far right-hand side of Figure 10 (A), the overall price action is bullish. However, another fact about this long tail candle is that for a period of time during the time period of the candle, the sellers were in control and trying to push the price lower. You won't know who these sellers are, but when you look at a chart that expands upon the time frame of this candle (for example, to cover a 24-hour period of time, there are 24 candles in a 1H (1-hour) chart but only 6 candles in a 4H (4-hour) chart), and you see several candles with the same type of behavior, i.e., a long tail at the bottom of each candle, you can speculate on the decision of the big players. It is likely that these big players are slowly sending the price lower and ensuring the retail trader's buy orders are being filled. This will result in the price jumping higher. Then, after some time, if these big players make their big decision to drop the price lower (which is not shown in this figure, but would present as a large bearish candle), there won't be many buy orders left on their way down because they have already consumed almost all of the buy orders placed by us retail traders. Scenarios like this will be discussed in Chapter 3 when I explain the price action in supply and demand analysis. My intention here is to emphasize the fact that each candle has a hidden story behind it which is worth dedicating some time and thought to.

In the following section, I will demonstrate how to use the drawing tools on the MT4 platform and I will add in some indicators that are often used by traders. If you are already familiar with the charting tool on the MT4 platform, or with other charting platforms such as TradingView.com, you can skip this section because it contains some very basic charting instructions.

Trendlines, level lines and channels

Perhaps the most important portion of your charting time will be spent on drawing (which is also known as plotting) trendlines, horizontal lines and parallel channel lines. You will see the use of each type of line in the trading systems explained in the next chapter, however, drawing these lines will be briefly discussed here. As you can see, Figure 10 (B) displays these three types of lines. As a novice trader, I found it very interesting to learn that the market moves in certain directions following a simple trendline or respecting a certain horizontal level line.

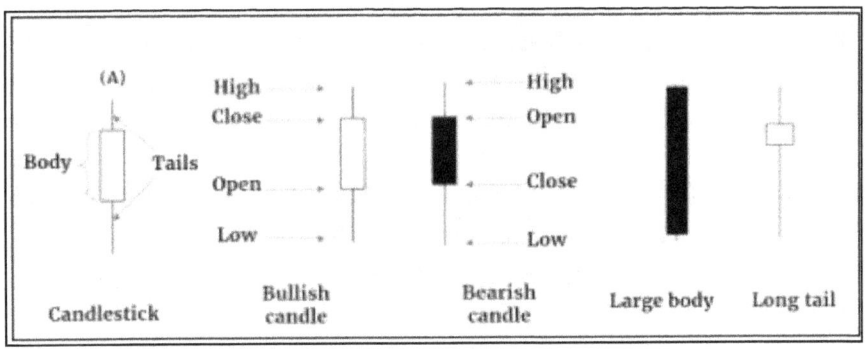

Figure 10. Examples of candlesticks (A) and drawing lines on a chart (B)

The first time I observed such a simple movement in the market, I thought buying or selling when the price touched a trendline or channel line would make me money. You can also notice how the horizontal line in this plot acts as both a floor and a ceiling over different periods of time. The concepts of "support" and "resistance" arise from such a simple reaction of the price to a horizontal level.

A closer look at the lines shows how a line is actually drawn. There are several ways to draw lines on a chart. As shown in Figure 11, two different ways of drawing result in similar sloped lines, yet different thought processes are involved.

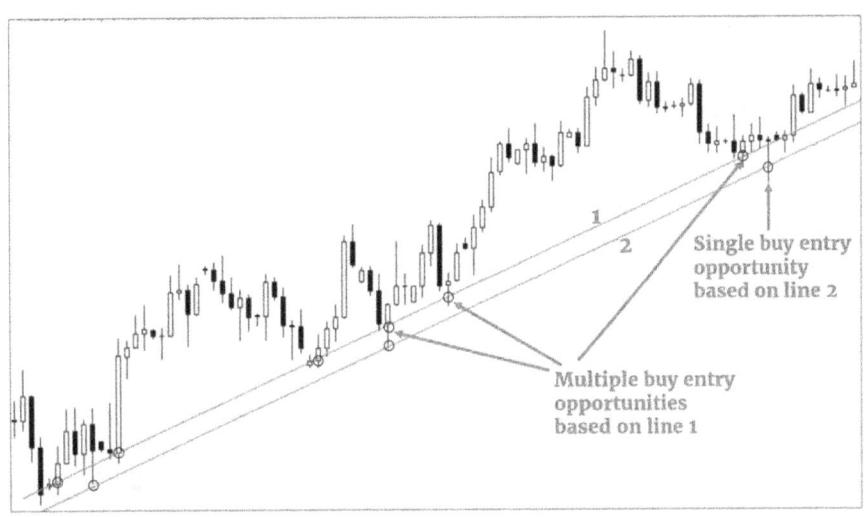

Figure 11. A method for drawing trendlines

In general, the trendlines and horizontal lines are drawn by connecting the minimum and maximum points in the past price with the anticipation of a future similar reaction in the price. However, it matters how you determine the minimum and maximum points. On a candlestick chart, the body of a candle represents the opening and closing of a price. The "wicks" or the tails represent the abrupt jump or drop in the price during the time period of the candle. It is believed that the more points a line touches, the stronger it affects the price once it comes back to it. As you can see, line 1 consists of at least six occasions where the body of the candle has touched the line. However, line 2 is formed by only connecting three points at the very bottom of the candle tails. Imagine that you wanted to place a buy order based on line 2. You would have only one opportunity to do this, and that would be in the third touch of the line, as the first two points were used to draw that line. On the other hand, you would have at least three opportunities to buy based on line 1.

Now let's discuss what line 1 represents: to avoid using the tails of candles to draw the trendline means that you decide to ignore the sudden reactions of the price to various factors in the market. These factors apparently have not been impactful enough to break the line. In other words, you decide to ignore the noise of the market. The body of a candle technically means the price range where the currency pair has lingered the most. The tails are the extremes of the price range in that day (or month, week, four-hour period, etc.) where the currency pair's reaching of a certain price (their "touching" of the trendline) was followed by an immediate reaction. These reactions are very important indicators. You need to accept the fact that the creation of an uptrend or downtrend is not the result of a few retail traders. The price will move in a certain direction because some big players in the market decide to step in and move the price to what they consider to be the fairest value. Imagine that you are one of these players, with "unlimited" access to money. You do not buy or sell at any price whatsoever just because you simply can. You want the best price and once you see it, you will grab it. The tails are the footprints of these players. As soon as their orders get hit, the reaction appears as a tail in the price. I will discuss more about this process in the next chapter. For now, I suggest you learn and practice by drawing some lines on your charts.

Indicators

Another set of tools are the indicators that are often used in the world of trading. As I mentioned in the previous chapter, I was fascinated by the power of some of the most complex indicators to accurately predict price movement. In the end, I was also frustrated by the contradiction in the prediction of price among some of these indicators. It seemed to me that the more I learned about these indicators, the more confused I became. I suspect that some of you could testify to having experienced the same feeling. My conclusion from using these indicators is that they only work because we the retail traders think they work and the big players want them to work. You'll read more about these conclusions I've reached in the next chapter.

To insert an indicator on your MT4 charts, follow the instructions in Figure 12. There are different categories of indicators including the trend followings, oscillators, etc. I will discuss some of the commonly used ones in the following paragraphs.

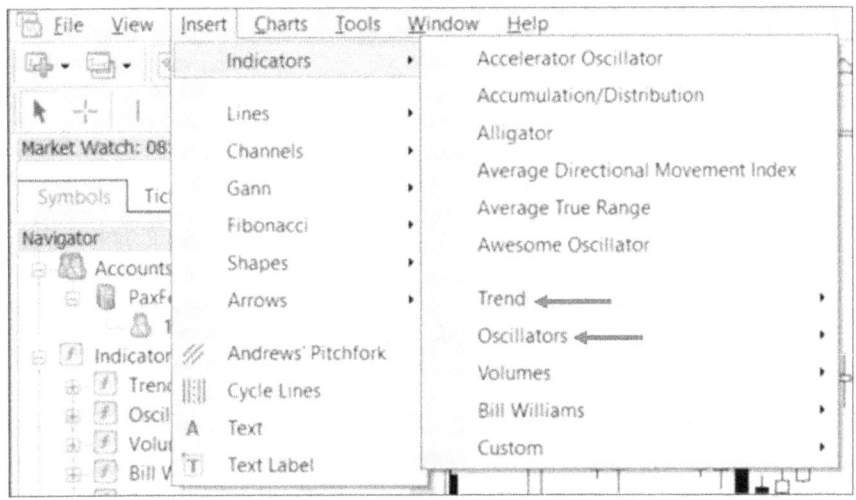

Figure 12. How to insert indicators on MT4

200-period moving average: The 200-period moving average is perhaps the most common indicator of them all. It is simply the average of the closing prices in the past 200 candles at any time frame. Because of its diverse use, it causes the price to bounce whenever the price comes close to it. Moreover, once the price moves through it, the trend seems to start reversing. Figure 13 shows an example of the price reaction to the 200-period moving average on the 4H chart (the 4-hour chart) of the EURUSD.

Figure 13. 200-period moving average

You can see how accurate this indicator is in predicting the price reaction. Again, this simple indicator works because everyone believes in its significance in the price action. It seems that there is a direct correlation between how common the indicator is and its strength in predicting the price movement.

Fibonacci: Another indicator which is very common among traders is the Fibonacci retracement indicator. It is inspired by the Fibonacci sequence, which is a series of numbers that appear unexpectedly in numerous patterns of nature. Figure 14 shows how this series of levels between two price extremes is predicting the price movement.

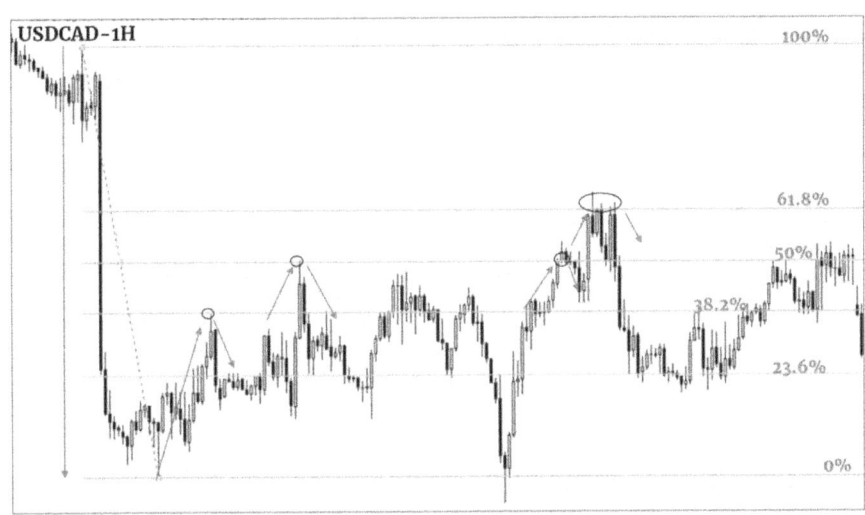

Figure 14. Fibonacci retracement levels after a big price movement

As you can see in this graph, the price shows significant reaction to the important levels of 38.2%, 50% and 61.8% retracement. This is a very common retracement behavior after a sharp movement in the price. The popularity of this single indicator among traders makes it important for you as well. There are many trading systems that utilize the Fib retracement levels along with simple support and resistance, trendlines, moving averages and such to predict the price reaction points. Start drawing some lines and combine it with the Fib analysis to see if you can come up with your own trading system. It will be good practice. More importantly, try to find the situations where it did not work and speculate about the reasons behind that.

Relative strength index (RSI): One of the most common indicators is RSI, which is in the family of the oscillators. This is an indicator that measures the rate of change in the price variation. It has a simple mathematical formula that uses the difference between the average amount of gains and losses in a certain past time period. The default time period is set to 14 on most platforms and is perhaps the most common time period used by many traders. The nature of this indicator is its repeating fluctuation between 0 and 100 (thus the oscillator title). However, quite often it fluctuates between the common values of 30 and 70.

Anywhere outside of this range is referred to as the "overbought" (above 70) or "oversold" (below 30) zone as shown in Figure 15. When the price reaches some extreme high amounts, the RSI enters the overbought region and buying is not recommended. The opposite is true when the RSI drops to below 30. It can be seen on this chart that solely relying on the RSI would have had good returns for a patient trader. However, quite often the RSI will enter the extreme region and stay there for an extended amount of time, during which the price will create higher values. This is referred to as a bearish or bullish "divergence" and it is often followed by a definite reversal in the price. It's important to note though that the reversal might take some time in a strong trending market. Hence, relying solely on this indicator could result in large losses before making any profit. Nevertheless, RSI is useful in combination with other indicators and trendlines to confirm the entry level. Many short-term and scalping trading strategies use RSI as one of their main tools.

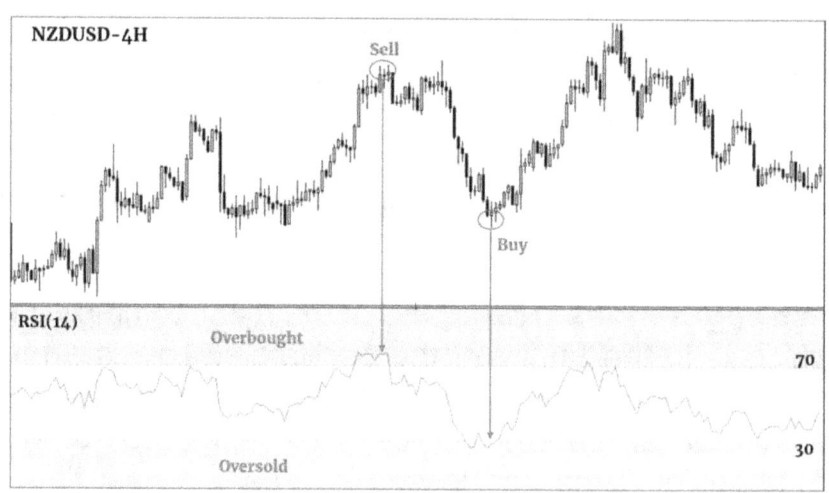

Figure 15. RSI indicator, with overbought and oversold regions highlighted

Stochastic oscillator: This is another popular oscillator indicator that measures the momentum in the market. This indicator compares the current closing price with the range of price in a specified period of time, which as mentioned above is 14 by default. Similar to the RSI, it signifies the overbought and oversold regions in the price movement. This is another indicator used by short-term traders to gain quick profits from the fluctuation of the market. Figure 16 demonstrates an example of the 5M chart (the 5-minute chart) and the stochastic indicator as the indicators for triggering the buy and sell orders. Again, it should be noted that this indicator will not perform as a stand-alone indicator. However, it provides useful information on the overbought and oversold regions.

Figure 16. Stochastic indicator

Bollinger Bands ® (at times referenced by traders as BB): Another popular indicator among traders, Bollinger Bands measure the amount of volatility in the market. A simple moving average and a certain standard deviation away from that moving average are used in order to determine the upper and lower bands. A look at the price movement of a sample currency pair shows the effectiveness of Bollinger Bands in predicting extreme high and low levels. Figure 17 shows an example of Bollinger Bands on a chart and how they could yield significant trading opportunities. Similar to the last two indicators, this is an indicator mostly used by short-term traders. The essence of this indicator is that periods of low volatility can be expected when the bands "squeeze" close to each other and high volatility can be expected when the bands move away from each other. It is usually recommended to use Bollinger Bands in times of low volatility and when the market is moving in a price range without a clear direction. While the expansion of the distance between the bands indicates high volatility, the bands cannot be used to predict the extent of that high volatility.

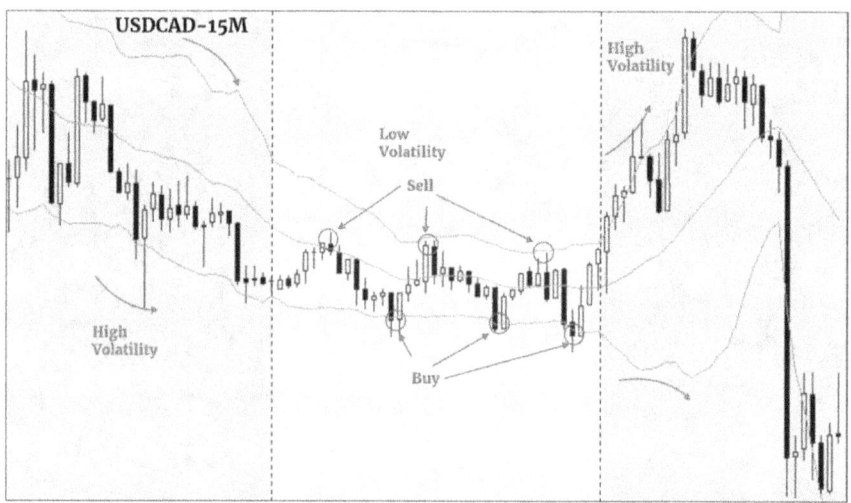

Figure 17. Bollinger Bands and their potential for identifying solid trading opportunities during a period of low volatility

The indicators listed above are only a fraction of what is available in the world of trading. It is beyond the scope of this book to discuss the details of all of these indicators. It is also not the intention of this book to promote any indicator over another. As mentioned in

Chapter 1, the excessive use of indicators was what caused me much confusion (besides the loss of my capital!). My research and practical experiences have led me to the conclusion that there is no one simple mathematical formula that is capable of predicting the sometimes rational and sometimes irrational behavior of human market participants. The market is a dynamic and ever-evolving environment that demands a trader's full attention and analytical power in order for them to survive.

Note: If you have skipped this entire section related to indicators and charting, I hope you read this statement: Do not expect any indicators to do your job for you, because they will not. However, knowing about these indicators will help in understanding the underlying origin of the price movement.

Swing trading vs. day trading

There are two general styles of trading, swing trading and day trading, and both are distinguished by their time periods. If you are new to trading, your idea of trading most likely is something close to the swing trading style. This style of trading includes buying or selling a security, a stock, or a currency pair over a relatively extended period of time. What is a relatively extended period of time? It depends. For a stock, a swing trade could take a few hours, days or even months. The goal is to benefit from the long-term swings in the price without worrying too much about the noises on the minute charts. A swing trader will open a trade with a defined stop loss appropriate to the trade time frame. They will perhaps check on the status of the trade once a day and analyze the market sentiment. In the case of a good opportunity, they will add to their position to maximize profit. They will eventually exit the trade once they have made their target profit. Does this style of trading seem interesting to you? Then you should definitely read more about it in your spare time. The methods in this book are mostly based on this style of trading. So, read on.

In the forex, a swing trade can last from 30 minutes to a few hours to a few days. "Position traders" are another category of traders who use this style. They add to their position along the way and watch the market carefully to extend their profit for months or even at times for as long as a year.

In contrast to the first style, day trading has different implications. For a stock trader, day trading means opening and closing trades in the same day, often within the first hours of the market being open. This is similar to "high frequency" trading, where the trader jumps in and out of a trade in a matter of seconds or minutes. This is a method for taking advantage of the impact of market volatility on high-volume stocks. There are pros and cons to both methods. Day traders are not worried about holding their positions overnight and therefore avoid the anxiety that typically results. In the foreign exchange market, day trading has a similar definition. Based on the time of the day, such as the London market, New York market or Tokyo market, the forex day trader chooses to trade only during these volatile sessions. They often open and close trades within a few minutes (usually less than an hour). A subcategory of the day trading style is "scalping". Scalpers are those who benefit from any small movement in the price action. Like high frequency traders, they enter and exit a trade within seconds and at most a few minutes. This style of trading requires a large amount of capital or leverage, besides uninterrupted presence in front of your trading station.

Both styles of trading have their own positive and negative aspects. My personal preference is swing trading because it matches my lifestyle and requires less intense and focused attention. I do not have to be constantly sitting behind my trading desk. I only need to revisit my charts on an occasional basis.

Volume

Before moving to the next chapter, it is essential to discuss the controversial subject of "volume". If you have an even brief experience in trading stocks, then, like me, you probably find this subject interesting. By convention, volume is the number of shares traded per a certain unit of a time frame. It is an extremely useful piece of information because it reflects the intensity and seriousness of a price movement. For instance, when a volume bar with 500,000 shares appears on the 5M chart of a stock with 10 million outstanding shares in the market, it signals that a big player has stepped into the market. It also means that a significant change in the fundamentals of the underlying company has occurred. Most likely, such a move will provoke several investors to want a portion of the action. And, as a day trader, that is the perfect opportunity to ride the rally and exit with a large profit. Of course, the mechanics of such a trade are more complex than the explanation given here. Moreover, several powerful indicators have been developed using volume as an input parameter. Many day traders perform their analysis and trades based on such indicators. The Volume Weighted Average Price (VWAP) is among the most popular volume-based indicators.

What about the forex? Is there a similar concept in the forex market? If you ask the MT4 platform, it will immediately say, "Yes, there is." You can simply add the volume by right-clicking on the chart and selecting "Volumes". Alternatively, you can add volume as a separate window underneath the chart using the "Insert" menu. In a naïve and intuitive interpretation, one might guess the volume on MT4 refers to the total number of contracts traded at a certain time. A closer look at the actual number could result in interpreting the number as a multiplier of 100 or 1,000, since the number should not be that small for such a huge market. Unfortunately, none of these "guesses" explain the true meaning of the volume.

As discussed in the previous section about brokers, the forex market is not a centralized market like the stock exchange is. Hence, the data from your broker's server provides only the information about the trades reported on their server involving their clients or their liquidity providers. It does not include any information from other brokers, ECNs (electronic communication networks) or the interbank market, which together are the major market movers. Moreover, the volume number on the MT4 platform is actually the "tik volume". A tik is the number of times where there is a new price quote being passed to the broker's server from their liquidity providers. The tik volume is the number of tiks received in a certain period of time. For instance, the volume number of 50 means that the platform received 50 price quotes during that given time. It does not provide any information regarding the size of the contracts traded during that time period. However, even the tik volume could be useful to track the times of high volatility. It has also been shown that the tik volume and the true volume are somewhat correlated. After all, it does show the level of activity in the market. Therefore, volume could be a useful source of information and, in fact, many trading systems rely partly on the volume number.

Trading community

Another factor that I would like to emphasize is the significance of understanding what other traders like you think about a certain currency pair or stock price. As a trader, you will very likely find yourself sitting behind a desk and staring at your monitor for hours without talking to anybody. You will then find yourself doubting and second-guessing your own thoughts and decisions. To shed light on these doubts, the first line of action is to seek the opinion of others. Readily accessible social media channels make it very simple to find answers for many of your doubts. I am not against utilizing social media for gaining more insight about the overall sentiment among traders. However, similar to the case of indicators, you will find "famous" traders and financial institutions contradicting each other and, in the end, creating more confusion. You need to realize that nobody should and will do your job for you. Just like I did, along with all of the successful traders I know, you have to learn the basics for yourself, develop your own strategy, go through real-time trades, and modify your method. There is no shortcut to this process. Once you find a reliable strategy that works for you and your lifestyle, you need to stick with it, build upon it and keep refining it. What you should not be doing is jumping without any rhyme or reason from one totally different strategy to another.

Let me share with you my experience with social media. Very often, I would find a trader with a working strategy who was gaining exciting profit. I would go back to my trading platform, use that strategy and end up losing more than winning. Frustrated from losing my money to a useless strategy, I would go back to social media and seek out more working strategies. I would find another successful trader and follow their strategy, which would result in another loss. I soon realized it was a never-ending cycle that had to stop. I had to break this cycle or else I would never succeed. I realized that I need to be the one developing my own strategy for me - and not for anyone else – and not from anyone else. I am certain that the strategies that those successful traders used were profitable for them. I just forgot the "me" element in the process of copying their strategies. "I" am not "them" and I think and make decisions differently from everyone else. I learned that whenever I see someone posting large profits, all it means is that it is possible for me to also make those kinds of profits. And let me stress the word "possible": it's possible for me to make those kinds of profits; it's certainly not guaranteed.

On the other hand, it is very useful to talk about your thought process and strategy with other like-minded individuals. I always use this example when I talk with my fellow traders. Based on my personal experience, whenever I want to learn something to perfection, I teach it to someone else. It is similar to talking out loud about your ideas with another person. It makes those ideas seem real and achievable. By hearing your voice explaining your thoughts, a different part of your brain gets activated and you ultimately receive more insight. Hearing what other people think also functions the same way. Very often, I discuss a trade with an experienced friend of mine, only to realize where I could have done better and what needs to be changed. A similar process happens when I suggest a trade idea to our community of traders and then listen to their opinions. While from different backgrounds and with quite varied approaches, we share and discuss ideas to improve each other's strategies. Online forex trading chatrooms and communities are great places to find experienced traders and useful learning tools.

The strategies discussed in this book revolve around deciphering the price action and observing the charts from the viewpoint of large institutional traders. Besides teaching conventional technical analysis, my purpose for writing this book is to build curious minds that search for the inherent psychological patterns behind simple price charts. Fortunately, there are trading communities offering useful advice toward achieving such a purpose. Among many, the "Set and Forget" website (https://www.set-and-forget.com/) is a good place to find like-minded experienced forex traders. Alfonso Moreno, the founder of this community, offers excellent advice and strategies within the realm of supply and demand trading. Another forex trading room with a more technical and day trading approach is the "Price Action Traders Institute" (https://priceactiontradersinstitute.com). Here, you get access to live daily trading sessions where you can see how the founder, Kim Krompass, and her colleague Kevin Hunt place their trades. Connecting with traders and mentors who share your trading platform and strategies, analysis methods, etc. (your "toolkit" so to speak) could be a critical step in your journey to become a successful forex trader.

As mentioned, I am also trading with a group of fellow traders who share ideas with each other and discuss anything and everything related to forex trading. I share my trade ideas with our community and explain the rationale behind each of my trades. I also share my weekly analysis of the major and cross forex pairs based on the actions of the institutional traders (just in case you don't recall, near the beginning of this chapter I explained the difference between major and cross currency pairs). This community has been built to assist individual traders like you and me to gain practical insight into the trading world. Traders with different backgrounds and skill levels gather around to help and learn from each other. Our community is already one of the world's leading destinations for stock day traders. We would like to expand this community to the forex market to accommodate traders who have a taste for forex and long-term strategies. If you would like to gain more insights about my trading strategy, ask questions and learn the process, you are more than welcome to join us at www.BearBullTraders.com.

To summarize, I believe there is a fine line between getting trapped in the noise of social media and utilizing it as a tool for improvement. Having a community of traders around you to whom you can ask questions will make the learning process more interesting. There are always traders who have been in this game longer than you have. Nothing replaces experience, so why not use it? Asking questions and seeking opinions from people who have already gone along the same path you are cannot do any harm. Just remember that you still have to make your trade decisions based on your own knowledge and analysis, and not because of an experienced trader's decision.

CHAPTER 2: FOREX TRADING SYSTEMS

Trading methodologies that work for me

My trading philosophy

I n this chapter, I will share a collection of trading systems that I have been using over the past several years. It should be noted that these systems are neither proprietary nor a guaranteed way to get rich. These are simply a combination of a few charting tools and indicators that have proven themselves worth trying. I developed these systems over a number of years through extensive experimentation and gradual modification along the way.

I want to begin my explanation by pointing out that I do not believe in a "golden" trading system that works for all trading styles and time frames. Over the years, I have tested and experimented with numerous methods I found online that advertised guaranteed profits. Although these systems caused me significant losses with only occasional profit, they did motivate me to dig deeper into the mechanics of trading. Today, I regard those losses as a worthwhile investment that has led to the profit I now make in my daily trading life. Before diving into the technicalities of these methods, it is crucial for me to elaborate on my point of view regarding the world of forex trading. I strongly suggest not skipping the next few paragraphs since what follows is truly the cornerstone of all of my decision-making when trading. Whether our viewpoints are aligned or contradictory, I hope the following commentary raises some questions in your mind about the driving forces in the market and how they function.

The methods explained in this chapter sometimes rely on the use of drawing tools, but they rarely rely on indicators. Their strength lies in the underlying mechanism and not in the indicators. With that said, the indicators are great tools to help keep you alert about the mindset of both retail and large institutional traders. Yet, there is an unwritten and significantly important difference between these two: the mind of a retail trader versus the mind of an institutional trader. Small traders like me, and perhaps you, are those who have the capability to enter and exit a trade in a matter of seconds. If we do not see a trade working as we expected, we can close the trade and move on to the next opportunity.

The big players, on the other hand, do not act and make decisions in that manner. Comparatively speaking, these are traders who have access to unlimited sources of money as opposed to our limited resources. Moreover, these big players are instrumental in decisions to alter the direction and valuation of a stock price or currency pair exchange rate, and they should thus be aware of any fundamental change or implication of such a change in the underlying currency pair. While they also speculate on the direction of the market based on their analysis and resources, it is their speculation that is what is actually driving the market. Even if they are occasionally wrong in their prediction, their decisions can still reverse the direction of the market. Regardless of the accuracy of their predictions, I would count on their educated prediction rather than mine. After all, they have access to the most recent and relevant sources of information. My purpose in explaining my opinions on the role of these big players is to lay out the framework for a better understanding of the trading systems set forth in this book.

Let me discuss further now the role of indicators, chart patterns and trendlines in the forex market. In my opinion, these points can be extended to any tradable asset. Over the past two decades, and especially following the advent of the internet as a public resource, the availability of information has become considerably more widespread and easier to access. Within the context of forex, people do not have to attend a four-year education program in order to understand the fundamentals of macroeconomics, nor do they have to attend the education programs of a financial institute to be able to start trading on their account. All of these traditional educational materials and opportunities to learn from the experts in the field would add to an individual's strength in the world of trading, and I am not against taking these steps. However, the internet is filled by great sources of knowledge which you can use in a targeted manner to learn about the subject area of your interest. For instance, you can find how to open a forex account with a reputable broker and start trading in a matter of minutes. You can easily find out how most successful retail traders think and trade either for free or for a fraction of the former cost.

Perhaps the most available and easy to access items are indicators, and you can learn about the mathematics behind them and how to use them effectively in your trading in just a few minutes. I used to think that indicators were the hidden secrets that big players used in their decision-making. I also suspected that the reason that they worked so perfectly and so often was because these big players used them. I then asked myself, why would they reveal their trade secrets to the public? My answer was that they probably could not control the flow of free information in the internet. My next question was, what would they do if everyone knew their secrets? Would they not use them anymore? To find the answers to these questions, I tried searching in every corner of the internet, and yet I found no answer. This is when I started creating my own interpretations and developing an understanding of how these big players make their decisions. Again, the following statements are my way of reasoning about how the world of trading works. I hope the discussion sparks some thinking in your own mind because that is my only intention.

To be able to answer my questions, some of which were mentioned above, I had to alter my mindset and get inside of the mind of an institutional trader. I read as much as I could and talked with other traders I knew in order to create a picture in my mind that was as accurate as possible. Imagine that you are an institutional trader who places big trades in the market on a regular basis. Beside the retail traders, your major competition is other institutions like your own. You have to create strategies and use your resources in a manner that benefits your own institution. In the world of trading, there are three fundamental decisions: buy, sell or step aside. The latter will not make you money and therefore is not an option for you as a big player. If you decide to buy a pair or stock, someone must sell it to you. In your particular case, someone with a large or "unlimited" amount of money can do that. If you have made the decision to buy something, other big players have most likely come to the same conclusion. This means you have to outsmart your competition by having a faster way to access accurate data, a faster internet speed, a larger number of traders working for you than for your competition (to buy on your behalf), and as many other advantages as you can think of. Your alternative solution is to convince a large number of retail traders to sell to you. The actual process is definitely more complex than this simple analogy, but let's go on.

The most efficient way to convince this "herd" of individual traders to place sell orders is to convince them that the currency pair or stock is not going up. The most available tool to do that is the common charting tools used by these traders. Let's discuss this in a simple schematic of a trending channel. Figure 18 shows a diagram of an upward channel that has been respected in the past. Retail traders would place their buy orders around point 1 to take advantage of the upward move. You as the institutional trader also want to buy at the best price. Because a channel has formed, you know that there exists a large number of buy orders at price 1. You also know that the retail traders place their stop losses near the prior low point to protect their account balances. As discussed in the previous chapter, the stop loss for a buy order is essentially a sell order. In other words, you have a large group of traders who are convinced to sell at a certain point. All you need to do is to use a small fraction of your unlimited money to drag the price below the stop loss area in order to buy all of these sell orders. However, the channel would have to seem intact in order for you to profit from your buy order. Your buy order will immediately push the price back into the channel and therefore the retail traders will enter back in on the way up.

What if you want to buy more? You know that there are lots of sell orders at point 2. To take advantage of the upward movement and maximize profit, you place another big buy order at that point in response to all of those sell orders. In this situation, the result would be a "breakout" from the channel, which is bullish. The breakout traders will then join the movement and push the price higher, only to maximize your profit. Beyond point 2, you start taking profit by selling to the upward movement. Alternatively, you could also start placing large sell orders to push the price back into the channel so that the channel seems intact. I hope this basic explanation starts to make sense at this point. I recommend re-reading this part if it is still not clear to you. For practice, you may replace the channel with another more complex indicator of your choice. The mechanics of the thought process for the big players and retail traders would remain similar to the above scenario.

It is quite possible that you yourself have considered this process of thinking in the past; if so, we have a common way of approaching challenges. As mentioned at the beginning of this chapter, the thoughts and systems discussed in this book are a collection of available information scattered around the internet plus the results of my own critical search for answers. I do not expect you to agree entirely with the mechanistic view outlined above. In fact, it took me years to convince myself. My intention is to both encourage you to critique your own method of trading and to help you re-evaluate your thought process. It is very likely that you have your own working methodology which requires equally sophisticated reasoning. If you wish, I'd appreciate hearing from you about that thought process, or about any other aspect of forex trading for that matter. You'll find my email address at the end of this book.

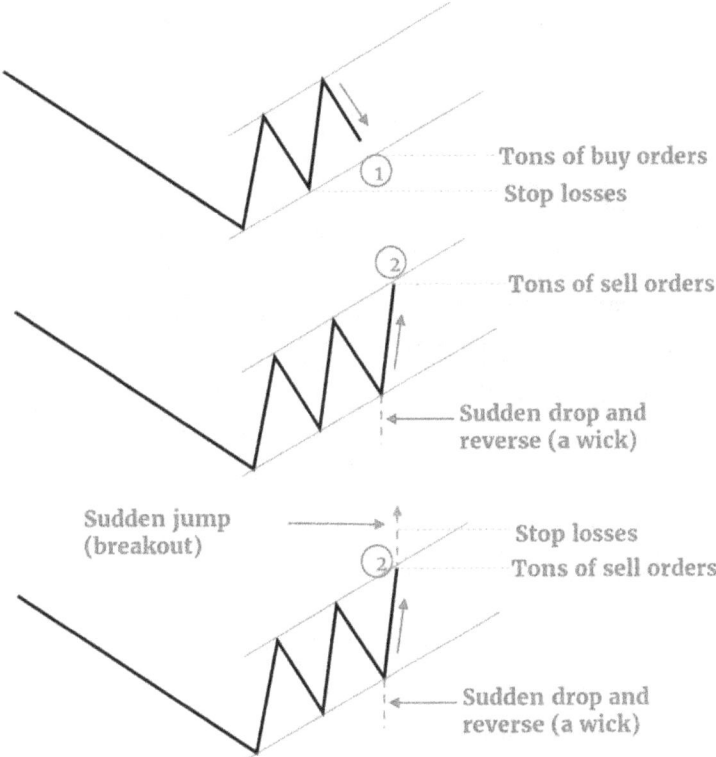

Figure 18. Mindset of a big player vs. small trader

As you can no doubt imagine, there is much more involved in the process of getting into the mind of a big institutional trader. In order to ensure this book is of a manageable length, I will end my discussion about this subject at this point. The next section describes the step-by-step procedure for taking advantage of some of the most popular trading systems that I also use in my own trading. You might have come across these systems in the past, and I must emphasize that these systems do not always produce profitable trades unless you understand the underlying mechanism and how it affects the price movement. Moreover, your predictions will remain true and relevant only as long as the fundamental driving forces remain intact. You must never forget that we forex traders always become aware of these fundamental changes <u>after</u> the big players, so staying agile and being willing to yield to these changes is the key to surviving in the market. I will explain more details about the concept of being agile toward changes in the market in the following sections.

Parallel trendlines or Andrews' Pitchfork

Trendlines are overrated! That is what you will most likely hear from any experienced successful trader these days, or from any traders who are using complex mathematical models to predict the next big opportunity. And you just heard it from me. Nevertheless, that doesn't mean they are not useful. If you are still not convinced about why I emphasize their usefulness, I encourage you to go back and read the previous section of this chapter about my trading philosophy. Trendlines still work because most traders in the market believe they work and also because the institutional traders want them to work. It is therefore essential for us to concede the fact that they are not to be ignored. However, there is a bigger concept which always holds true, whether or not you personally believe in trendlines. It is that the general direction in the market will always be bullish, bearish or neutral. If you open a chart of any tradable instrument, you should be able to identify its direction. If you see the market is making higher highs and higher lows, you could easily say that the trend is upward. In such a market, buying that instrument is what the "herd" of traders is focused on. Trendlines are the creation of the general sentiment in the market, regardless of the direction.

(For your information, "higher high" is a term used to describe when the price moves to a new level higher than its previous high, and "higher low" is a term used to describe when the price moves downward to a low level which is still higher than the previous lower price level.)

Within this concept of market direction, you can always find lines that seem to be respected by the price action. From the early days of trading, it became clear to some of the great minds in the financial market that the price will swing between high and low extremes but always come back to a "median line". Alan Andrews was among the first who systematically studied this concept and created a system based on Newton's law of action-reaction. An engineering graduate from MIT, Andrews compiled his observations of the market movement with those of others like Roger Babson and George Marechal. In its core, his method relies on the role of a median line which seems to have an imaginary gravitational force over the price. Babson described the area below and above the line, respectively, as the times of depression and prosperity. Beside the median line, Andrews assigned two other parallel lines above and below the median line as the location of market extremes. Through extensive and elaborate experimentation, he demonstrated how such a simple, yet effective method can predict price movements. He developed an entire course on the concept of a median line and it sold for about $1,500 during the 60's and 70's.

Andrews' method relies on three major pivot points. These three are the price points where the market has shown significant reversal behavior. To be able to draw the parallel lines, three consecutive pivot points must be identified. The sequence is in a high, low, high or a low, high, low configuration. By now, his method has become very popular among traders, and I have been amazed by its power in predicting the price behavior in the market. I started my own analysis of this method because I had seen how it could result in profitable trades. However, before it became profitable, it caused me a significant amount of loss because I was solely focused on the line and not on the bigger mindset of an institutional trader. There is certainly more background about this method and its history, and I encourage you to read about it.

As mentioned, the lines are constructed based on three pivot points. Nowadays, any charting platform will allow the user to draw these lines based on choosing these three points. Figures 19 and 20 show two examples of this method in, respectively, a bullish and bearish market. Although originally developed for the daily charts, I have found this method is also applicable to 1H and 4H charts (1-hour and 4-hour charts). In my personal experience, I have mainly applied this method for longer-term trading rather than for short-term trading (which is what day trading is). Even for longer-term trading though, I still use the 1H and 4H charts as my preferred time frame for monitoring price movement and plotting my strategy. As can be seen, the three points in an uptrend are selected in the order of low, high, low. As Figure 19 shows, the bullish trend in the EURJPY over an almost nine-month period in 2014 can be rationalized using this system. The opposite is true for the case of a downtrend. The construction of the lines in the final drawing resembles a pitchfork and hence the term "Andrews' Pitchfork" was coined.

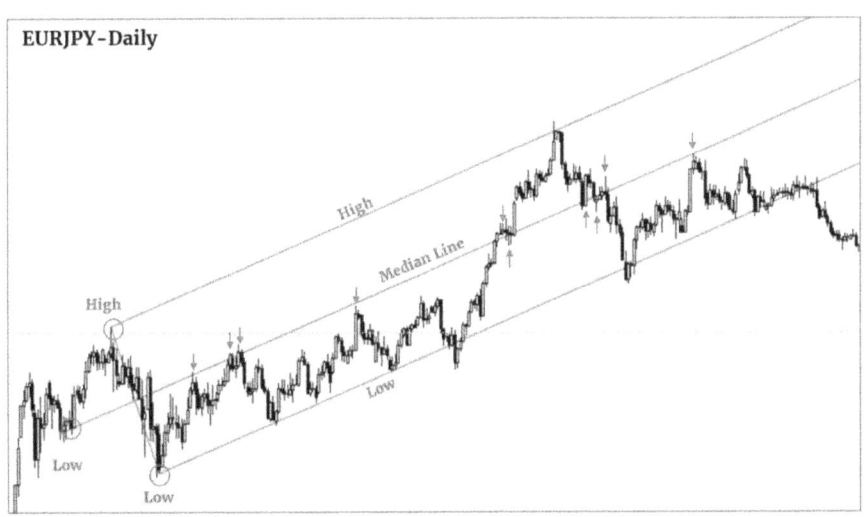

Figure 19. Andrews' Pitchfork representing bullish EURJPY market

Figure 20. Andrews' Pitchfork for bearish NZDUSD market

As mentioned, the market can be in a neutral status from time to time, but a median line acting as a magnet for the price still exists in such market conditions. The horizontal maximum and minimum extremes are also present, as can be seen in Figure 21.

48

Figure 21. Horizontal median line method for EURNZD

As you can see in all of these examples, along with many others you can find online, the Andrews' Pitchfork model provides a reasonably fair prediction about the reversal points in a trending or neutral market. Seeing the potential, I started drawing these patterns on my charts and traded based on the prediction of the parallel line method. It quite often resulted in a loss exactly before the price took the direction I expected. A closer look at any of the examples on the charts above reveals why this happened. As I discussed at the beginning of this chapter, the behind-the-scene fundamentals are the main driving force for the price movements. In an upward-trending market, such as that depicted in Figure 19, both institutional traders and retail traders recognize the uptrend, the difference being that the latter group does this earlier than the former group. To be able to enter in at the fairest price and profit from this uptrend, the institutions must take any opportunity of a price pullback to enter. Once they enter the market, the result is another upward movement. At the same time, they would require a large number of sell orders to satisfy their large buy order. Hence, they might find these opportunities by targeting the stop loss orders below trendlines. This will create a very short spike down in the price where retail traders would be stopped out before the next move up.

Please take a moment to look back at these charts and notice the spikes. As you can imagine, the selection of the pivot points is a somewhat arbitrary process resulting in different sloping in the lines. Regardless of how perfectly one draws their lines, the spikes in the price will always be there to take advantage of the stop losses. More importantly, drawing a perfectly aligned pitchfork based on the past price data does not make me (or anyone else for that matter) a successful trader. If anything, it only makes me an expert in drawing parallel lines on a chart.

Step-by-step thought process for planning and trading

In the following paragraphs, a step-by-step explanation of the procedure and the thought process during a simulated trading experience using the Andrews' Pitchfork method is demonstrated. My intention is to take you through a real-life example in terms of what I look for on a chart and how I implement this method. Based on past experience, I mostly use this technique on 4H and 1H charts to take advantage of the starting of a trend reversal. I do not predict the reversal with this method; in fact, I ensure that the reversal occurs before drawing my pattern. Figure 22 shows an example of a trend reversal which seems to be taking place on the EURUSD 1H chart.

Figure 22. Early detection of the break of a downtrend

As this figure shows, the occurrence of a double bottom at the right end of this chart is a signal for a reversal in the trend. (In case you are not familiar with the term, a double bottom occurs when the price bounces off of (or moves up from) a certain level twice.) At this point, you would like to observe another indication of the change in the sentiment of the market. This could be at the break of the down trendline which can be drawn using the high points in the past. This is shown in Figure 23 where the trendline from the left of the chart is now broken by the strong movement in the price. Upon observing such a strong signal, you would use the three pivots shown in Figure 23 to draw the Andrews' Pitchfork.

EURUSD-1H

Downtrend break → use
3 pivots to draw the fork

High

Low

Low

Figure 23. Break of the downward trendline to confirm the end of the downtrend

With the pivots shown in Figure 23, the fork can be drawn. This is illustrated in Figure 24 where the entire drawn object is removed, and all that is left on the chart is the image of a fork. From this point onward, you need to pay full attention to the response of the price to the extension of the fork in order to confirm its significance.

At this stage, you would like to first confirm the "magnetism" power of the median line. This means that any approach toward the median line should face some support. Likewise, once the median line is broken, you would expect the median line to act as a temporary barrier. Overall, you would look for buy opportunities in the regions below the median line and sell opportunities in the regions above the median line. Then, once you have defined the new trend in the market, you have to look for the big player, which will most likely enter the market as a buyer. Again, it is essential in any trading strategy to look at the price action from the mind of a big player.

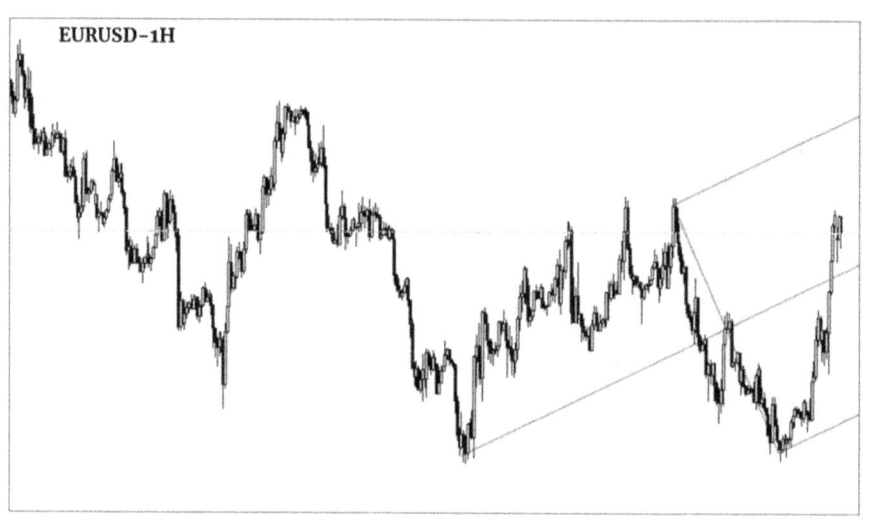

Figure 24. The median line and parallel lines drawn based on the trend reversal confirmation

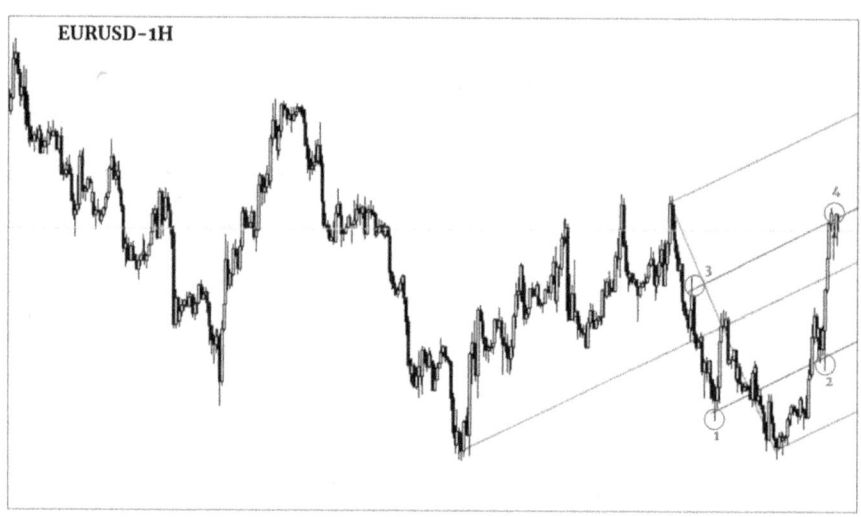

Figure 25. Identifying the big players' footprints

Figure 25 demonstrates the same chart with some additional annotations. As discussed earlier, the institutional traders make detectable appearances whenever they enter the market. These are points at which a strong opposite movement has caused a local change in the direction of the market. The institutional trader will always choose the most profitable price for their entry. Notice points 1 and 2 on the chart in Figure 25. The appearance of the long tail along with a sharp reversal in the price indicates big buy orders. If these traders still want to enter the market as buyers, they will not want to let the price go down all of the way below their previous entries. They will most likely place their buy orders according to the location of their previous buys. Please note though that this is not always the case. It all depends on whether they have taken their profit by placing large sell orders before reaching the parallel line based on points 1 and 2. Similarly, in the region above the median line, you should look for the big players' footprints for possible sell entries. You can see where I've marked in this Figure 25 a possible parallel line based on points 3 and 4.

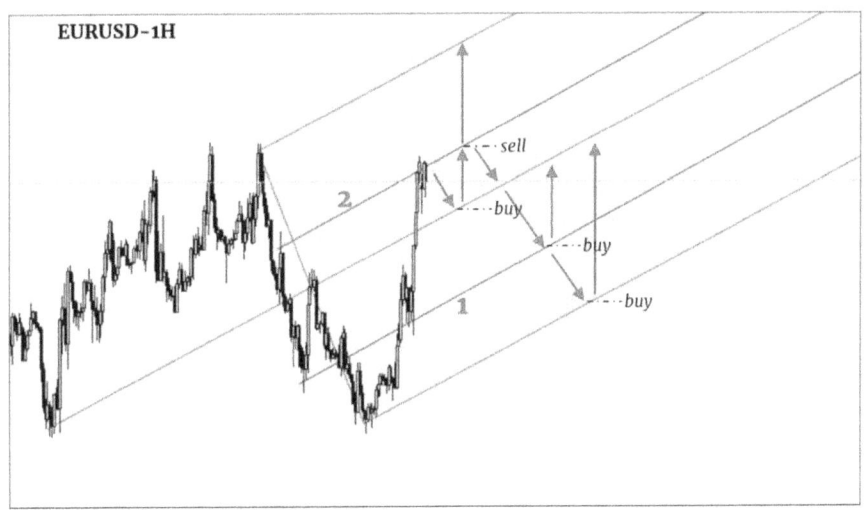

Figure 26. Making predictions based on the current price action

Based on the information available at the time, I would make the initial set of predictions as seen in Figure 26. I would place my buy and sell orders according to these predictions. However, any change in the price movements in terms of observing large institutional orders will have to be accounted for in the planning from now onward. Figure 27 shows the first movement in the price, which demonstrates how the median line, as predicted, will act as a support. An important parameter in a live order is your expectation or target profit. I would not expect the price to immediately break line 2, which is a strong barrier for the price. Hence, that line should be the first target profit. The other important parameter is the stop loss. I used to place my stop loss at a certain distance from my entry to control my loss. However, I was often stopped out of a trade due to neglecting the mechanism in the price movement. If the support line was broken with a strong movement, but without any signal of retracement, I would manually close my trade for a loss. This method required my full attention to the chart and I had to of course be present at the time of such movement.

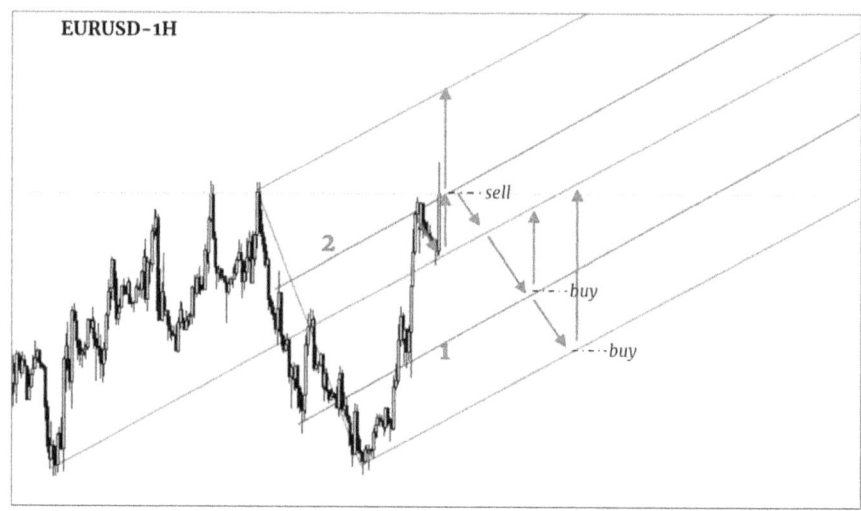

Figure 27. The first reaction based on my prediction

Figure 27 shows the first reaction to my prediction. The price does not go below the median line, so I buy at that median line and take my profit at line 2. My next prediction is to sell at line 2 and take my profit around the median line. My subsequent prediction is for the median line to get broken, then I wait for the pullback to the median line, and then I sell at the median line with my target profit at line 1.

My next prediction will be to buy at line 1 and at the low line of the pitchfork.

Figure 28 shows the price reaction to the resistance line 2. As per my prediction to sell the pair at line 2, the price sharply dropped right after the previous upward candle. Again, my target profit for the sell order has to be at the median line since it is acting for the time being as a support level.

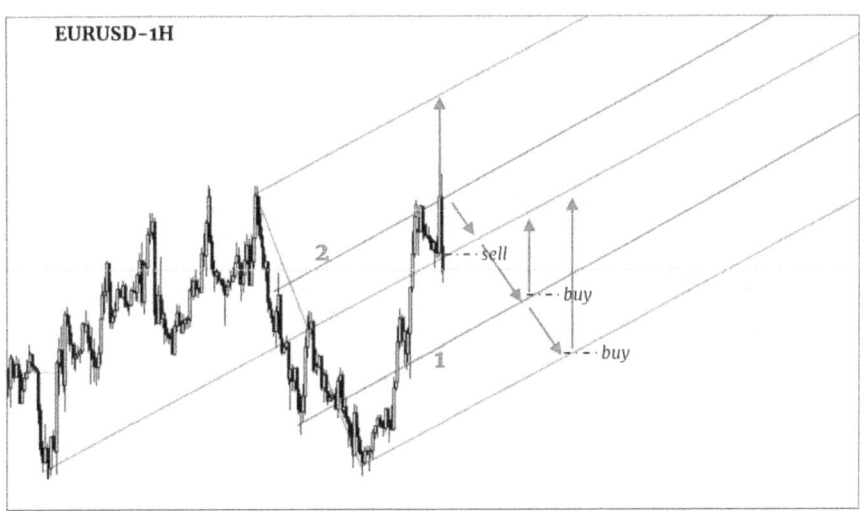

Figure 28. Second prediction based on resistance line 2

As the chart in Figure 28 shows, in addition to the fulfillment of my sell order when it reached its target profit, the price has broken the median line. This is due to the strong downward momentum in the price from line 2, which has completely wiped out the buy orders in the previous candle. This is the indication of a move caused by a big player who entered the market at line 2. At this point, I am looking for both a sell opportunity at the median line, and a buy opportunity below the median line around line 1. Remember, the price is in the region below the median line. Therefore, there should be more bias toward buying as the price moves farther away from the median line.

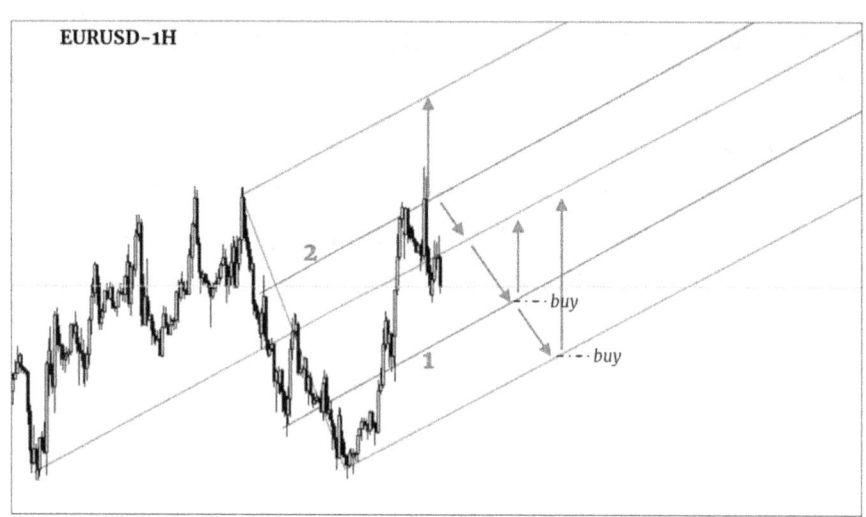

Figure 29. Continuation of the predicted price action

As Figure 29 shows, the median line has indeed turned into a resistance line, with the price showing a strong reaction to it. At this stage, I hope the process of placing limit orders based on these predictions has become clear to you. For the sake of brevity, I will present the results of these predictions in chart form until a major change in the big picture has occurred. Figures 30 and 31 show the development of the price action below the median line. In Figure 30, the first reaction to line 1 is a sharp upward movement. However, as Figure 31 shows, that movement did not follow through and my buy trade was stopped out at breakeven (which is often abbreviated by traders as "BE").

Figure 30. First buying opportunity around line 1

Figure 31. The break of the low parallel line

At the time of Figure 31, the price seems to have broken the low parallel line, which is supposed to act as a strong support level. Looking closer at the first reaction to the line indeed shows its strength as the price retraces back above the line. However, the occurrence of a continuous downward movement seems to be consistent with the breakdown of the low parallel line. At this point, I have to stay out of the market until a firm indication of the big player appears in the price action.

Figure 32 shows that there exists a strong movement upward, judging from the appearance of a strong upward candle. In fact, the size of such a move is the largest over the past few days. And by now you should know who can make such a difference in the direction of a market. At this point, it is safe to place buy orders near the low parallel line. Why?

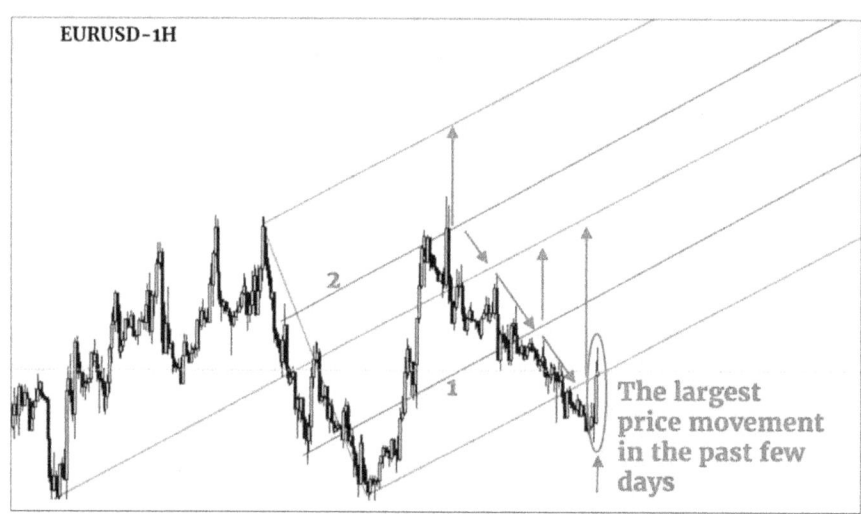

Figure 32. The appearance of large price movements caused by big players

It is safe to assume at this point that the institutional buyer created the big move shown in Figure 32 in order to defend its position and even add to it as the price lingered around the low parallel line. After all, the potential for the upward movement toward the median line cannot be ignored. Due to the possibility at this point of a market crash further down the road, it is essential to place a firm stop loss for your buy orders. Where would you put your stop loss? At this point, you should not intend to stay as a buyer if the price makes another low below the spot where the institutional buyer had stepped into the market. I hope it is clear now that once you find your big player, you can rely on their knowledge and power over the market. As an aside, by market crash I mean another sharp downward move which causes a breakdown of the previous low points in price, thus changing the overall perspective of the market participants. Let's move on to the next step of the process.

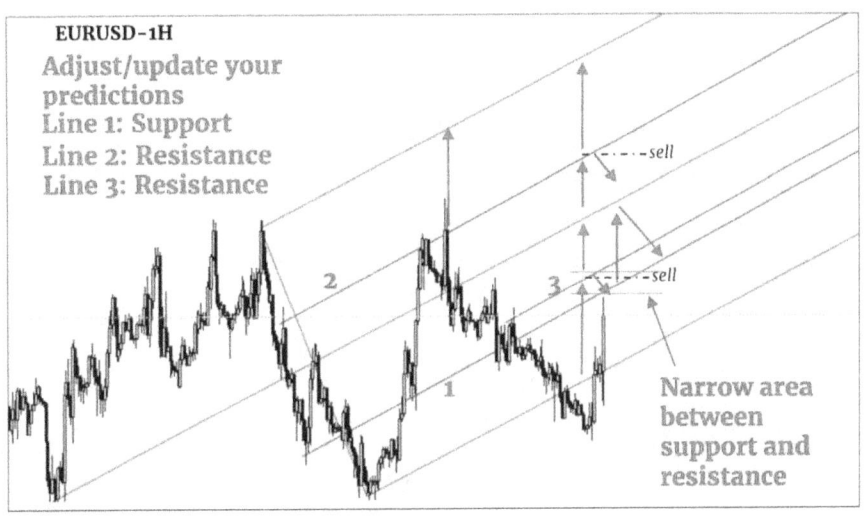

Figure 33. Adjustment and updating of the trading plan

As can be seen in Figure 33, the big player indeed did what I thought they would: that is defend their position and most likely add to their position, as shown by a sharp downward tail and then the strong move up. At this time, you will have to update your trading plan and make new predictions based on the previous interactions in the market. As this figure shows, the most interesting item is the addition of a new resistance line 3 to the chart based on the past tail in the original candle. Although you would expect a resistance at this line, you are still in the below-the-median regions, and that means you should be looking for buy opportunities. Moreover, you should realize that your expectation for a sell order on line 3 is very limited because the old support line 1 still exists. I would therefore suggest trading very short term near line 3 to keep away from being stopped out and incurring unnecessary losses.

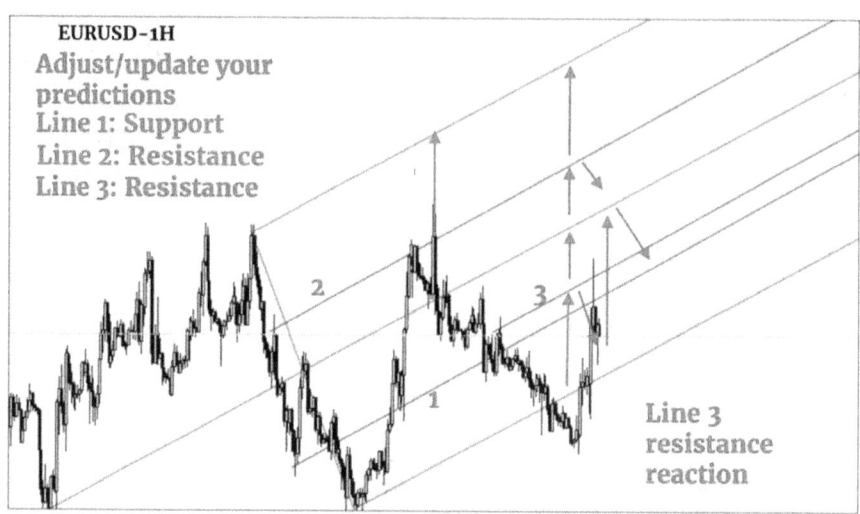

Figure 34. New resistance line reaction

As expected, line 3 has been proven to act as a strong resistance and the price has immediately retracted back from it. At the same time, line 1 did not act as a significant support line, as the price has broken through it. The appearance of a tail at the last candle shown in Figure 34 suggests the entrance once again of the big buyer into the market. Therefore, it is relevant to add another support line originating from that tail. For the sake of simplicity, I will not draw such a line as it is very close to the lower parallel line.

I hope by now you have become familiar with the thought process that must accompany the technical analysis of a chart based on this trading system. It is crucial to pay close attention to the footprint of the institutional traders because you always need to be on their side. Figures 35 through 39 represent the continuation of the EURUSD pair as it travels through the predicted pattern. I would strongly recommend you study each chart and observe my updating and adjusting of my trading plan and predictions. It is a powerful exercise to understand the details of each decision and each modification of my market prediction.

Figure 35. New resistance line based on prior price action (don't forget that BE stands for breakeven in trader jargon)

Figure 36. Breakdown of the median line, possible support opportunity on lines 1 and 4

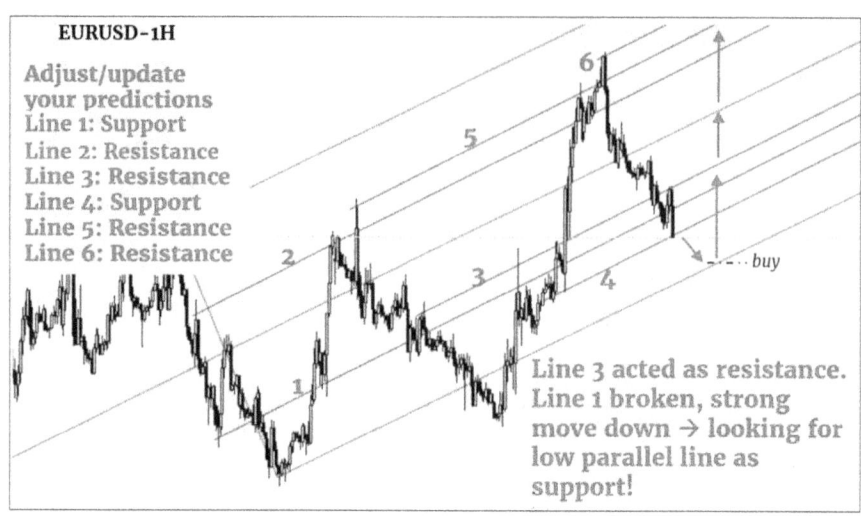

Figure 37. Line 3 resistance, strong move down aiming for the low parallel line

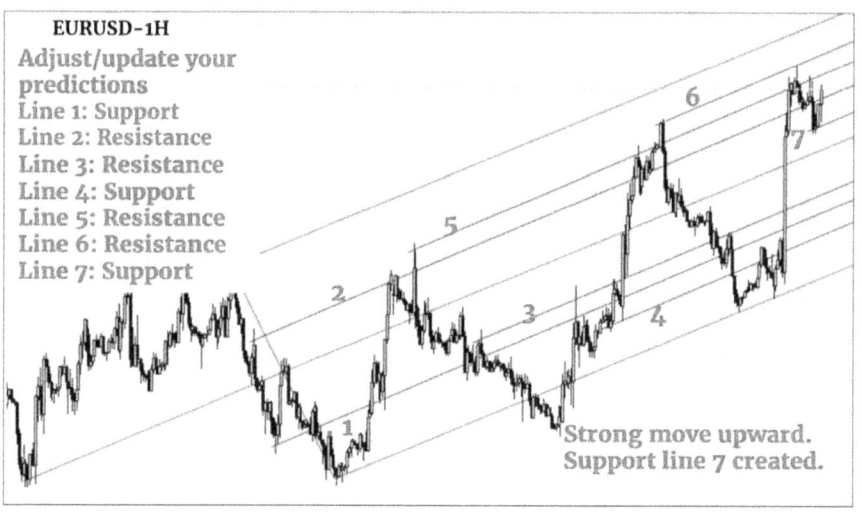

Figure 38. Strong move from the low parallel line breaking all resistances, line 6 resistance, new support line 7

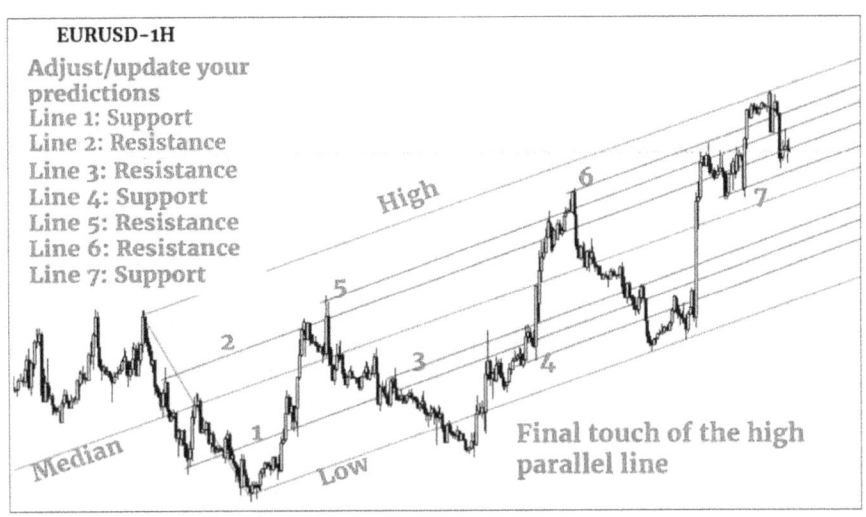

Figure 39. Final reaction to the high parallel line

Mark up the trading plan

As can be seen in the sequence of the above figures, there was a continuous dynamic evaluation process of the price action as I moved along the parallel line series. It should be noted that these are my decision-making processes during the actual time of these events a few months ago. It is essential for you to look back at your trades and mark up the mistakes which have caused losses of opportunity. An example of the markup process I used on my chart can be seen in Figure 40.

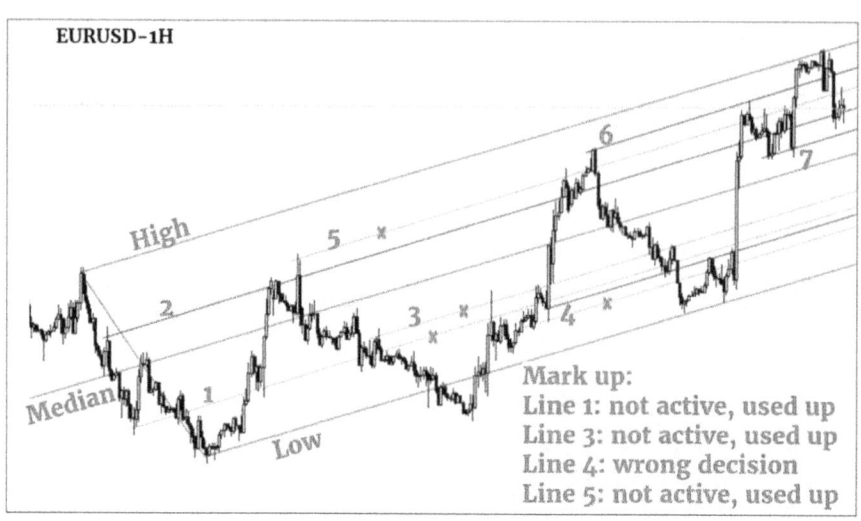

Figure 40. Markup process for the previous trades and line adjustments

As this figure shows, there are several key points that arise from this simple markup process:

- During actual trading, you need to be continually evaluating and re-evaluating the strength of each support and resistance line. I have grayed out those lines that seemed as the trade unfolded to become no longer active. This is due to the fact that once a level has been used more than two or three times, it is most likely not useful anymore. It is referred to as a "not fresh" level in trading jargon. The freshest level is the best level to trade from. As this trading progressed, you should have grayed out line 1, line 3, the original line 4, and line 5. (For those of you who are reading a paper copy of this book rather than the e-book edition, the reference to "grayed out" may not be that clear in Figure 40. These four specific lines present as slightly faded in the paper copy of my book and are marked by "x" signs).

- Looking back at line 4 reveals that I had originally placed it in the wrong location. The more correct way is to draw a line from a strong move away from that level. Notice the new location of line 4 on this marked up chart which is slightly above the original line 4.

- It is most beneficial to keep this general thought in mind: you should look for buying opportunities in the below-the-median line region and selling opportunities in the above-the-median line region. You will notice on the charts that the returns from selling in the buy region or buying in the sell region are very limited.

There is always more to the decision-making process during the actual time of trading when candles are being printed on the chart. This book is only intended to introduce a trading system that has resulted in profitable trades for me personally. Have I always won in my trades? Have I lost in any of these trades? "No" and "yes" are my answers to these two questions. Trading always involves winning and losing, but there is more to gain than just making money, especially at the start of your trading career. And what might that be? It is to build a strategy that you are confident in and to gradually over time start making more winning trades than losing trades. I have realized that I should trust my trading plan more than anything else. If I am able to develop a plan and, more importantly, track the big player, I am most likely right. This means that it is not the time to exit a trade if the big player is still in it. The proper use of a stop loss, and sometimes not using a stop loss, is the key in this process.

Remember: you always need to be thinking about the amount of risk you are taking in return for a reward. This is what is referred to as the "risk/reward" ratio in trading, and in any other investment activity for that matter. If the risk and reward are not clear to me before entering a trade, I do NOT enter that trade. Risk/reward analysis will be discussed further toward the end of this chapter. For now, I encourage you to take some time to identify the risk and reward in the trades I walked you through above based on the EURUSD Andrews' Pitchfork example. Try to understand where and why you would place a specific stop loss.

As you can probably imagine, I could discuss the details of many trades that I have taken using this simple yet effective strategy. This book though is intended to show a larger picture rather than strictly focus in on pure technical trading systems. It suffices to say that I have had many successful trades based on this strategy and that the thought process behind each trade has been somewhat similar to what I discussed in the above section. I do not expect you to start trading based on this system right after reading this part of my book. Instead, I strongly recommend that you open up charts on your platform and try to follow the same decision-making process explained in this section. As I mentioned, this method is mostly applicable to daily, 4H and 1H charts. That means it could be applied to both major and cross pairs because it does not depend on volatility and trading volume. Soon, you will find out that there are not too many situations where you could identify a pitchfork and benefit from it forever. The market dynamics, as well as macroeconomic events can impact the validity of this system. There are several criteria that I have mentioned in the first section of this chapter that need to be satisfied before developing your plan. What does that mean to you as a trader? It means once you find a working pitchfork, do not ignore its power and significance. Make your best effort to take advantage of its potential. And again, I would urge you to always keep your eyes open to observe the actions of your big trader counterparts, because most of the time those are the decision-makers.

The following section describes another trading system that I actively use in my daily trading. It will be helpful for you to understand the concepts and know-hows I have explained regarding the Andrews' Pitchfork methodology before moving on to the next sections.

Supply and demand trading

Demand drives the price up and supply pushes the price down.

There is not much more depth to this basic concept in economics. Supply and demand are the sole driving force for any movement in the market, be it the forex or stock market or the grocery market near where you live. Once there is a demand for an item, its price will move up until there is a sufficient supply of that item. The oversupply of the item will eventually push the price down. This process simply repeats itself. Before moving into the concept of supply and demand in forex trading, I would emphasize that this is a concept that has been around since almost the beginning of trading transactions by human society. A quick internet search will bring you thousands of webpages explaining this simple concept in various ways. All that is needed in this section, however, is the opening statement: "demand drives the price up and supply pushes the price down". If you search online, I am certain that you will find the related materials explaining the basics of this method, just as I was able to. The key here is for me to make the point that supply and demand is and always has been the only reason for any price movement. And believe it or not, I had forgotten this rule till long after I had started trading. So, please regard this section as a reminder of a simple rule that affects our daily lives virtually every time we spend some money, whether we are buying an iPhone from an Apple Store or apples from a grocery store, or even sending our kids to the neighborhood daycare. Supply and demand has implications in all of our lives even though we sometimes totally forget about it, or sometimes even try to fight it.

To be fair, my view of the market changed when I first started learning more about supply and demand and its role in the market, and this might happen for you as well. After losing my first real account almost 10 years ago, I thought that I was doing something seriously wrong. I had read every book and gone through every tutorial to make sure I was set for making money in the market, and yet I lost money. Concluding that I did not know the fundamentals of the market, I went to a university library and picked up an economics book. I should mention that reading a textbook was the only way I knew how to learn things in those school years. There were lots of irrelevant subjects explained in that book, but one topic stuck in my mind: the forces of supply and demand in the market. I did not look back at that book nor did I take any further action after that library visit. Over the next few weeks though, I found myself noticing the keywords "supply and demand" on numerous webpages and forums about the forex market. I did not know back then what was happening, but I later found out about an interesting phenomenon known as "heuristics and biases". My mind had become biased toward these keywords (supply and demand) and my eyes were picking up on them wherever they appeared. You might have had similar experiences from time to time. My purpose for writing this chapter is to change your trading mindset and the way your eyes see a chart. As I always say (maybe others have said it too, so please do not quote me on this), there are things that you cannot "unsee" once you see them! So, let's begin.

Note: As much as possible, I would rather use more pictures than text to explain the concepts in this chapter because that is how I learned them.

Step-by-step walkthrough: change how you see a chart

I begin with a simple candlestick chart. The chart in Figure 41 is the 4-hour chart of the GBPUSD pair at a randomly selected time in the year 2011. I would like to ask you to list the interesting and notable facts about this chart. Is there a particular candlestick pattern or trend you observe on this chart? The first obvious fact to me is the development of an uptrend move toward the right side of the chart. In addition, a possible double bottom formation is beginning to form in the center of the chart. There is not much else I see on this chart. Perhaps some indicators and a bigger picture or a higher time frame will tell more about what might happen next.

Figure 41. GBPUSD 4H chart from 2011

On the chart shown in Figure 42, I selectively highlighted in blue a few candles, while all of the other candles have similar white shading. No special indicator and merely simple code were used to highlight these nine candles. (For those of you who are reading a paper copy of this book, the reference to blue highlighting will obviously not present. The nine specific candles I highlighted will appear black in your version of book.)

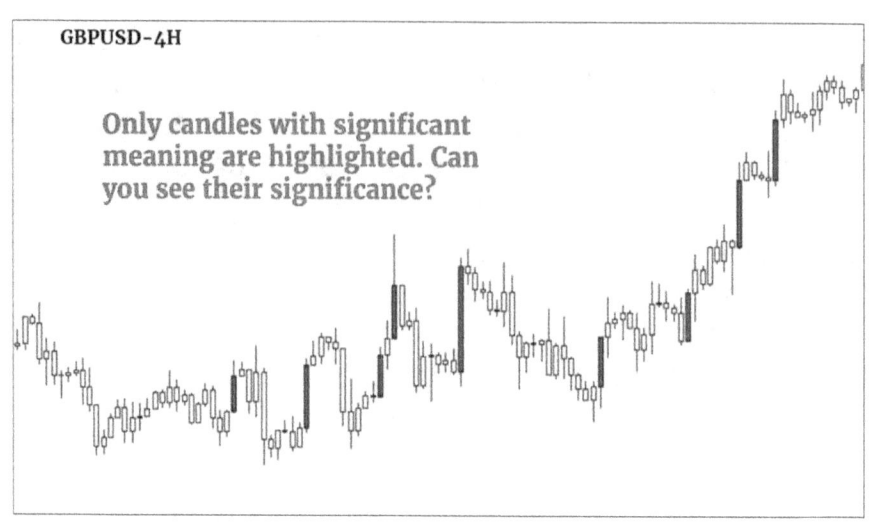

Figure 42. Highlighting a few candles

Before moving on to the next chart and my explanations, I would like to ask you to examine this Figure 42 and rationalize the significance of these blue candles (black in the paper edition of this book). I would suggest you jot down your thoughts before moving to the next figure. The first time I did this practice for myself, several "irreversible" processes occurred in my mind. I am quite sure that some changes will happen in your way of seeing this chart as well, should you be new to the concept. Now let's move on.

Figure 43 contains the same chart as in the previous figure, but with some additional annotations. As can be seen, the highlighted candles have some common features:

- These are among the largest upward candles and show a significant increase in the price during the four-hour duration of the move.

- With the exception of a handful of them, the body length of these candles is almost identical to the entire range they represent, i.e., open-close is almost equal to high-low.

- The price seems to have a similar reaction whenever it reaches back to where the blue candles (black in the paper edition of this book) began.

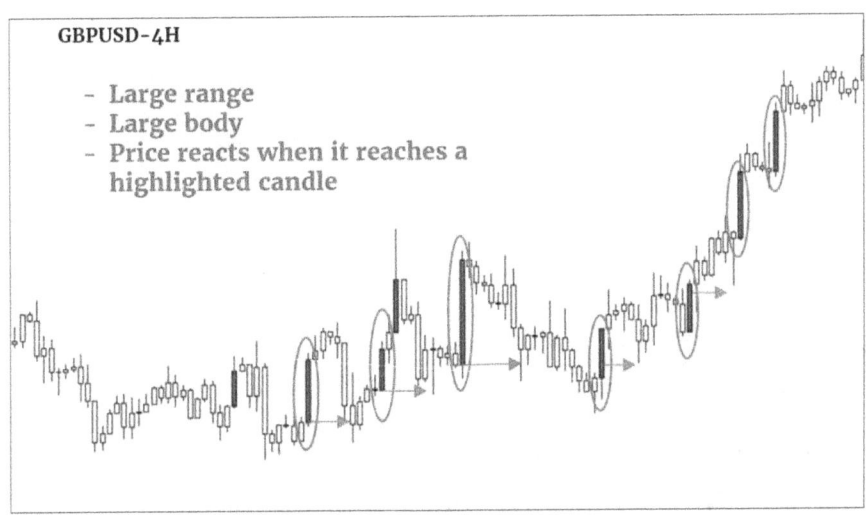

Figure 43. Annotated version of chart in Figure 42

I'm inclined to describe my first impression of such a simple price behavior in relation to these candles as "overwhelming", but I am not sure if that word describes it well enough. It might not look significant to you at the moment, but let's continue the exercise, and perhaps by the end of it you will be as impressed as I was. Based on what you just observed and the relationship between the blue candles (black in the paper edition) and the price, try to guess where you would place your buy order. In fact, try to place your buy limit order by drawing some imaginary price level. Now let's move on to the next figure.

Figure 44. Predicting based on the past highlighted candles

Was the dashed line in Figure 44 your prediction for the buy limit order? What was your reason for selecting that level? I encourage you to place another imaginary buy limit order based on what you see on this chart. In the next figure, I will demonstrate my prediction and its final outcome.

Figure 45 (A) and (B) shows my prediction for the next buy order and how that then performed in the future. Do you start to see some significance in these blue candles (black in the paper edition of this book) yet?

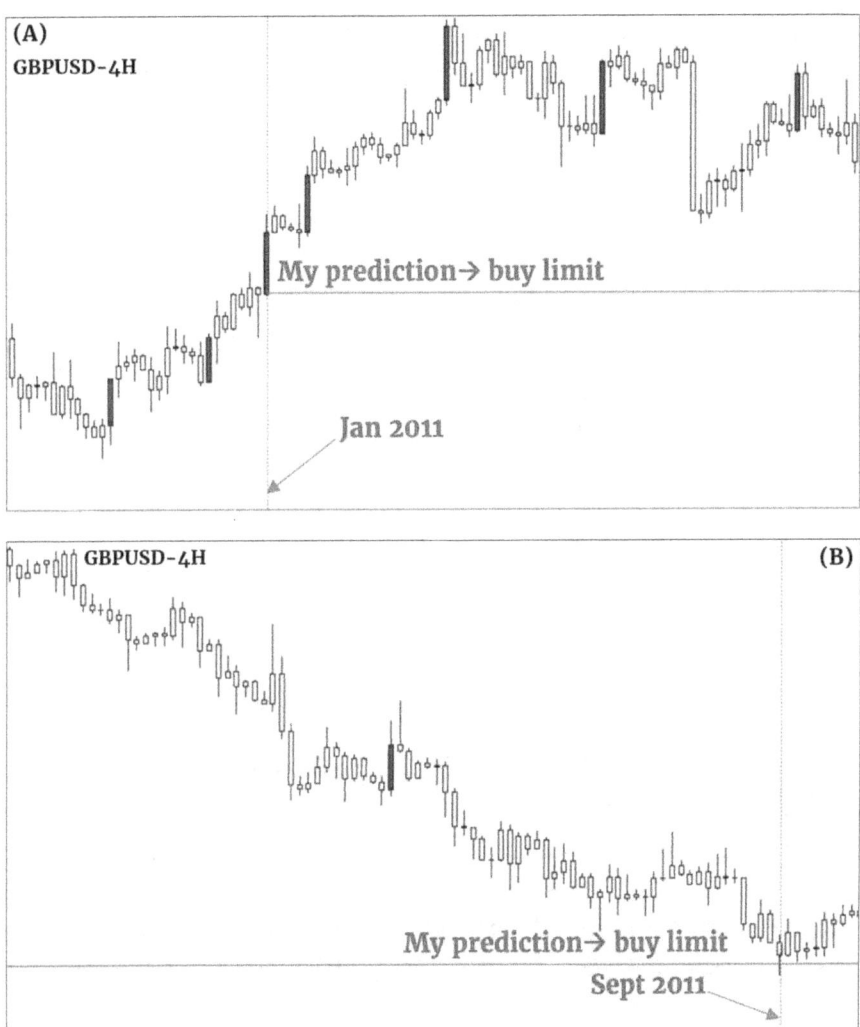

Figure 45. Buy limit order (A) and how my prediction performed (B)

I would not jump to any conclusion at this point. All you can say based on these few charts is that the price seems to be influenced by the location of these big candles. It also seems that the price is more impacted on its way up than on its way down. That can be attributed to the fact that these are large bullish candles and therefore they have a more powerful impact in a bullish trend. Let's continue this exercise with the other type of candles, the bearish candles. Figure 46 shows a randomly selected duration of an 8H USDCAD chart.

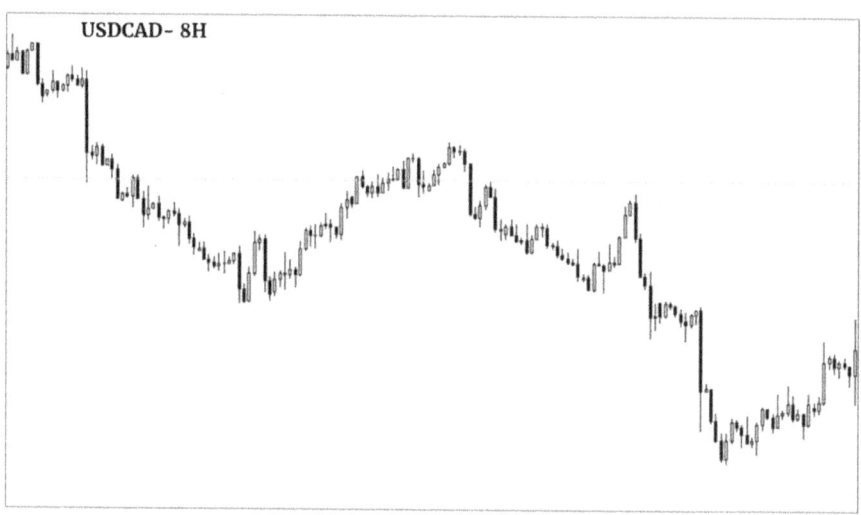

Figure 46. USDCAD 8H chart

Before moving on to the next figure, let's observe the prominent feature of this chart. When you went through the previous exercise, you might have noticed some features that you had not seen before on other charts. That was the case for me when I went through a similar exercise. Overall, this Figure 46 chart looks bearish. The trend can be represented by the trendline and perhaps a channel. Now, let's look at Figure 47, which is the same chart, only with some highlighted candles.

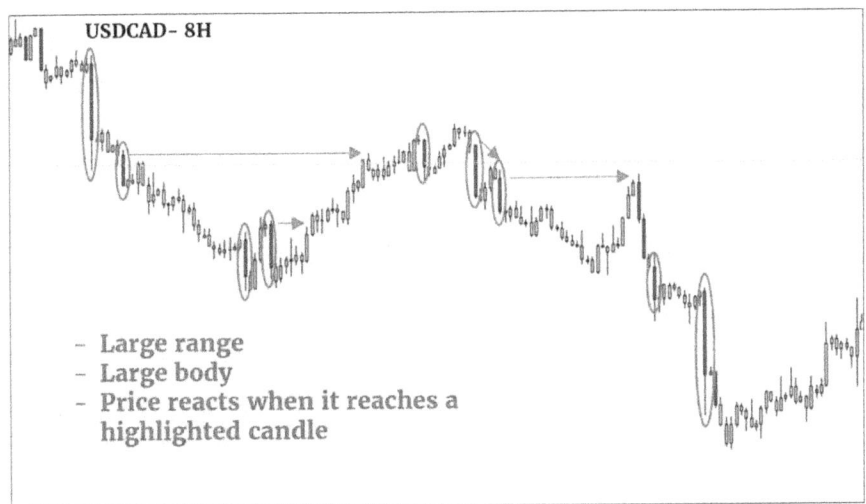

Figure 47. Candles with significant meaning highlighted

Similar to the chart in Figure 43, this chart also shows large body candles which seem to affect the price reaction once it reaches their level. As with the previous example, let's predict the next level where the price will be showing some reaction.

Why some levels do not work? Zone vs. level.

Figure 48 (A) demonstrates the three prediction levels based on the large red candles (black in the paper edition of this book) that envision that a price reaction will occur. The results for the reaction of the price to levels 1 and 2 are shown in Figure 48 (B). As can be seen, the levels drawn on the chart did not perform as expected. It seems that the conclusion based on the previous exercise is not accurate after all. This is the place where I could say, "I wish the life of a forex trader was easier." Instead, let me say, "This is not the time to give up on the finding. Let's dig deeper to find out why the prediction did not perform."

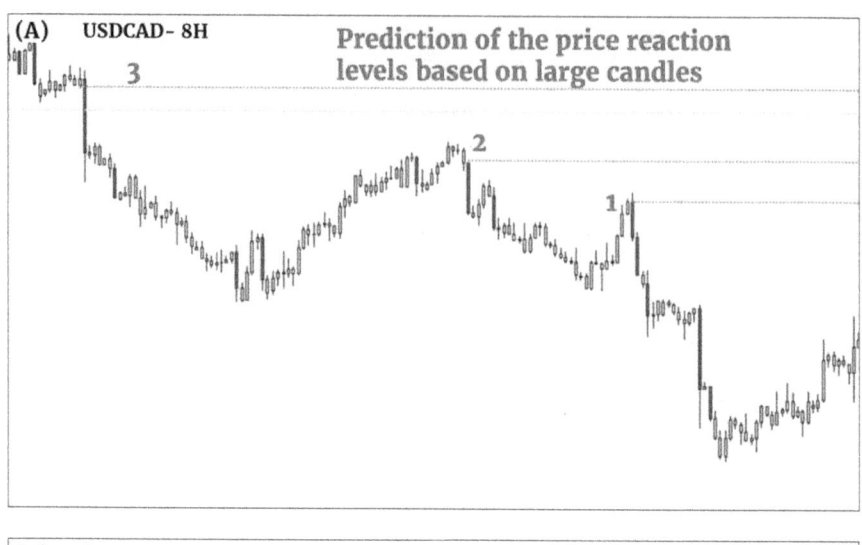

Figure 48. The prediction (A) and the performance (B) of the price reaction when reaching the levels of the large candles

A careful look at price behavior near level 1 reveals some interesting insights. The price at level 1 is followed by two large consecutive candles. In fact, I can assume that you might have selected the price level at the top of the second candle as your first prediction for the price, and, as you can see, that level also did not perform well. However, look to the right side of the chart where the price comes near the area in-between the top price of these two candles. It seems that the price reacted to that area not once, but twice, before it broke through level 1. This is illustrated in Figure 49 by drawing the price range rather than a single level. At this point, the conclusion can be modified. The large candles create a price range, or a "zone", where the price could show reaction to it once reached. Furthermore, the number of times that a zone acts as an active trade area is limited. You cannot expect the zone to induce reaction to the price forever.

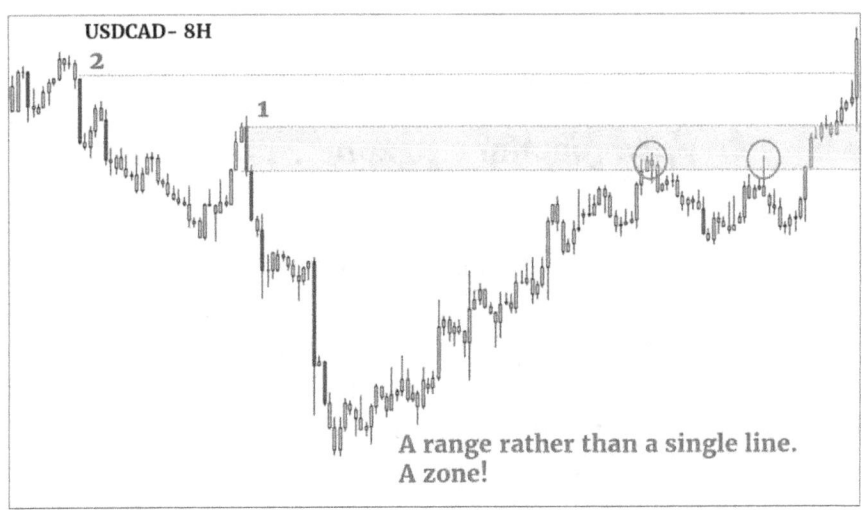

Figure 49. The price reacts to a zone rather than to a single level

Let's expand on the notion of a zone rather than a single price level to analyze the price reaction to level 2 on this chart. Similar to the previous zone, let's draw a zone using the large candle near level 2. This is shown in Figure 50. You'll see that the zone already induced two price reactions before the large upward candle at the right end of this chart broke through the zone. You can say that the zone in level 1 was a reaction to zone 2, and this is what is referred to as a "zone on top of a zone".

Figure 50. Two price reactions to zone 2 before its break on the third attempt

While drawing zones in the manner described above seems to result in some good trades, it has a significant drawback. The zone is too large. It requires a lot of capital and patience for the price to show the expected reaction to these zones. This can be minimized by considering the use of smaller time frames. It also highlights the importance of proper risk/reward analysis in trading. Let's look at this zone 2 in the smaller time frame of a 4H chart. Figure 51 shows that the large candle on the 8H chart consists of two candles on the 4H chart (2 x 4H = 8H), one of which seems to be significant.

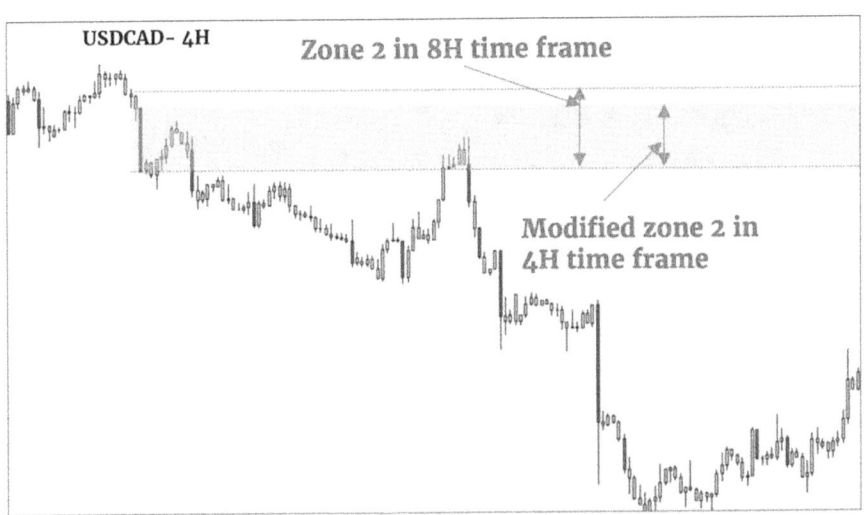

Figure 51. Modification of zone 2 based on the 4H time frame

Based on the location of the large candle on the 4H chart, zone 2 can be modified to expand over a smaller price range, as illustrated in Figure 51. You can assume a lower price risk using this smaller zone. However, it should be noted that the excessive use of multiple time frames can also be misleading. As a rule of thumb, you only need to look at three time frames to analyze and identify the zones. This will be discussed toward the end of this chapter.

Let's continue this exercise by looking at the third price level shown in the prediction set out in Figure 48 (A). The chart in Figure 52 shows the reaction of the price on the three occasions that it reached level 3. In this case, the single line level has already performed in the direction of this prediction. One can imagine that this level showed extreme strength, because it rejected the price three times.

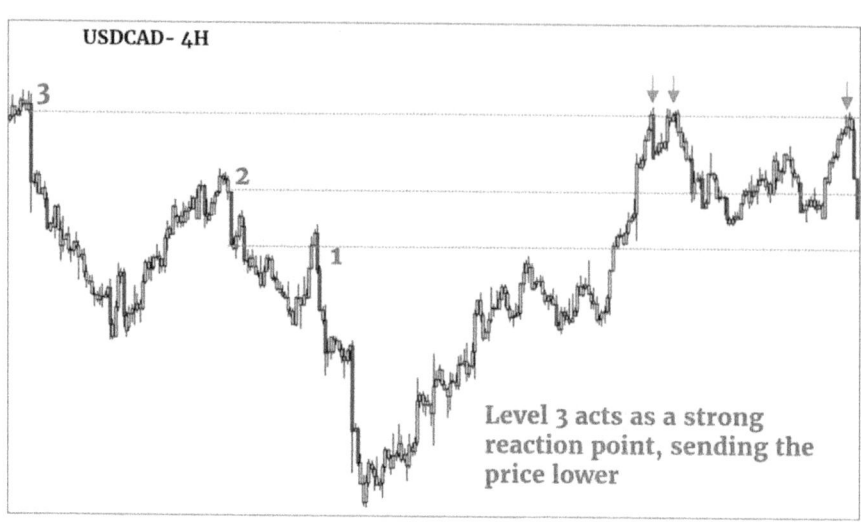

Figure 52. The rejection of the upward price movement when reaching level 3

If you were to expand the concept of zone to this level, two possibilities can be envisioned. These two scenarios are depicted in Figure 53. As can be seen, the first scenario shows aggressive trading behavior where the entire range of the candle at level 3 is considered as a selling zone. Following this approach, at least five price reactions could have been captured. These are shown by arrows in Figure 53 (A).

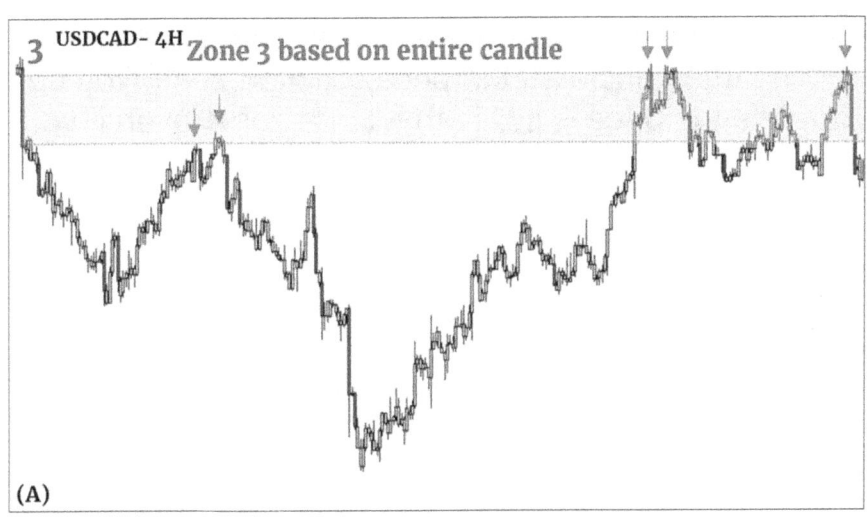

(A)

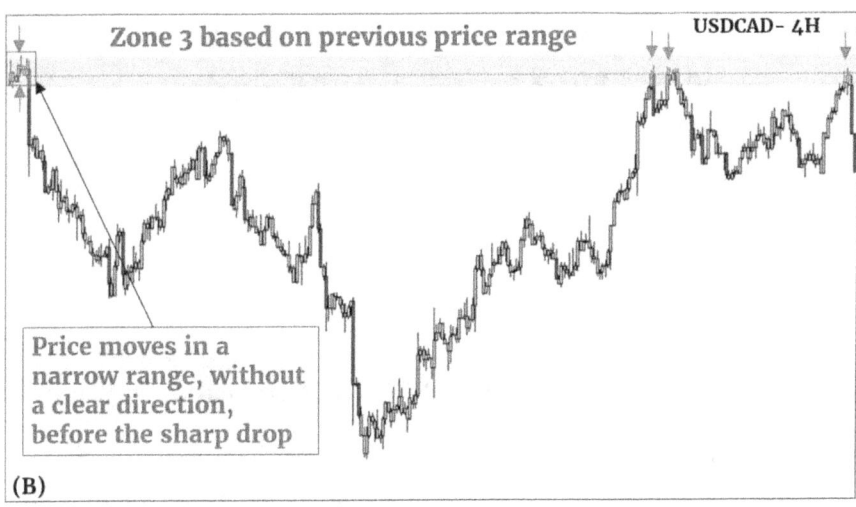

(B)

Figure 53. Determining the sell zone based on (A) entire candle range and (B) prior price range

On the other hand, if you use the previous price movement shown by the two arrows and a box at the far-left side of the chart in Figure 53 (B) (before the large candle), a narrower range can be drawn. Before considering the concept of risk/reward analysis, you should decide which approach is the most suitable for you. In other words, you need to understand how patient you are willing to be until the trade goes in the direction you anticipate. If you consider the entire range of the large candle as the price reaction zone, you cannot exit the trade while the price is still in that large zone, even if you are in a loss.

The competition between the bears and the bulls

Let's continue this exercise by looking at both types of price reaction, bearish and bullish, on the same chart.

Figure 54. The competition between the bulls and the bears

As Figure 54 shows, the chart contains both blue candles (flagged with upward arrows) and red candles (flagged with downward arrows). (If you are using the paper edition of this book rather than the e-book edition, the colors will obviously not present, but the arrows pointing upward and downward will.) You will notice that all of these candles are of a significant size. Please take a moment to examine the strength of each candle in terms of predicting the price movement in the future. Do all candles predict the price movement correctly?

The answer to the last question is "no". There are some candles on this chart that, despite being significantly large, do not produce any price reaction. In contrast, other candles predict the price reaction accurately and, in some instances, even predict it correctly more than one time. What do these differences tell you about the significance of each candle? The following section is another viewpoint to add to your mindset from this point forward. It will help you to see another level of price behavior when looking at any chart.

Strength of levels

Please look back at the chart in Figure 54 and identify the candles that bear the most significant reaction related to the price. It is very likely that these candles have broken a significant level during their formation. On the other hand, those candles with less impact on the price have failed to break any significant price level. Figure 55 shows the candles that have broken or failed to break the previous significant level. The price reaction to each of these selected candles is also shown.

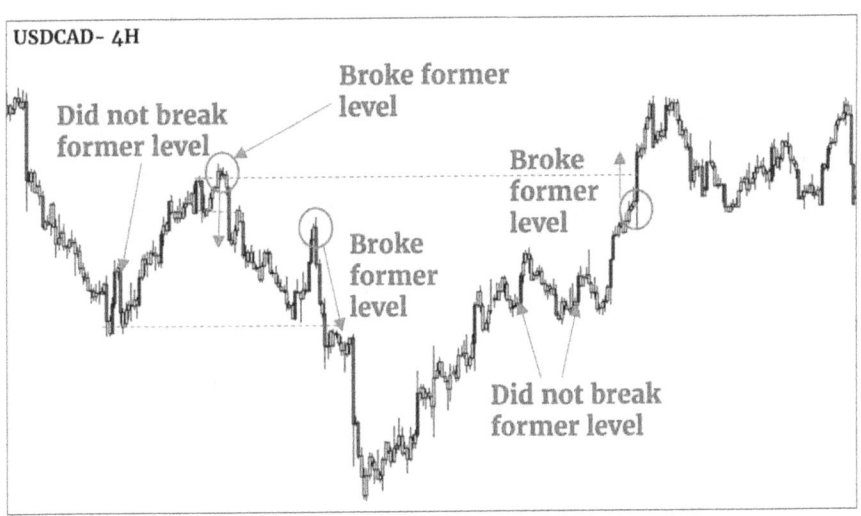

Figure 55. Strength of levels based on large candles

As mentioned, the levels and candles on this chart are only a small selection of the competition between the bears and the bulls in trying to overcome the previous levels. Overall, those candles that have been successful in overcoming a significant price level seem to perform better in the future as a price reaction location. This is another thought process when looking to identify the level to trade from in the future.

Practice: Based on the information discussed so far, I recommend that you go through a few charts on your platform and try to make predictions for the future price reaction. In your demo account, place a few limit orders and observe their performance in the coming days. For starters, I also recommend avoiding zones that have been used in the past. The concept described in this chapter so far can be applied to any time frame as long as a series of **high**, **medium** and **low** time frames is observed. Decisions on the time scale depend on your goals and availability. For instance, I prefer 1D-8H-4H and 1D-4H-1H as my time frame series. This allows me to check back and modify my trading plan once or twice a day.

Filled and unfilled orders

The previous sections were mainly focused on the importance of the large candles. In most cases, this is all you need in order to make your trading decisions. If you went through some practices on your demo account, you most likely found the power in following these large candles. Let's discuss now the mechanics "behind the scenes" of these candles and why they are significant. As mentioned in my trading philosophy, I strongly believe that retail traders are not capable of creating such large candles. These price movements are usually created by the orders of the big players in the market. This is where the concept of supply and demand becomes useful. It is the *imbalance* between the supply and demand that moves the price in a specific direction. A **supply zone** (abbreviated as SZ in the figures that follow) is where the price drops due to the large number of sell orders. A **demand zone** (abbreviated as DZ in the figures that follow) is where the price starts to move up due to the large number of buy orders.

The opposite of this scenario is when there is a balance between the supply and demand. During the balance time, the buyers and sellers are in equilibrium, and both agree on a common price. This is the time when there is no significant movement in the price and can be seen in the schematic of Figure 56 by the green shaded area. (If you are using the paper edition of this book rather than the e-book edition, the three large shaded areas in Figure 56 will present as three large light gray stripes.) On the other hand, once this balance is violated, the price moves according to the winning side of the equation. In this case, the sellers have decided that the price is not at its fair level and should be lower than the price in the balance zone. Hence, they flood the market with their oversupply of sell orders, which forces the price down.

The price drop can be created by a set of big players who have decided to lower the price based on their analyses. However, the execution of all of their orders must happen at a price that is profitable for these sellers. It means that most of the sell orders by the initial sellers are placed near the top of the candle. The rest of the traders, and perhaps other big players, will then follow these sellers to push the price down. It should be noted that the big initial sellers have the largest impact and control on the price because they have managed to reverse an upward movement, or disturb a price balance zone, with their orders. To bring the price down, they had to place a very large number of sell orders in the balance zone. It is very likely that many of these orders will not be filled due to the fast departure of the price from the balance zone. In other words, the "*filled*" orders drive the price down, while the "*unfilled*" orders are kept there to be filled if the price moves back up.

In most cases, the balance zone is the price the big players were willing to pay to drive the price down. Unless a fundamental change occurs along the way, they will still be willing to pay that price, and the unfilled orders will remain untouched. In addition, the other big players who have been left out are likely to be interested in entering the market around the same level. As a result, they will also place their limit orders near the beginning of the large movement in price. This is also where you, as an individual swing trader, want to be placing your orders. You do not want to be the one who sells at the bottom of a price drop.

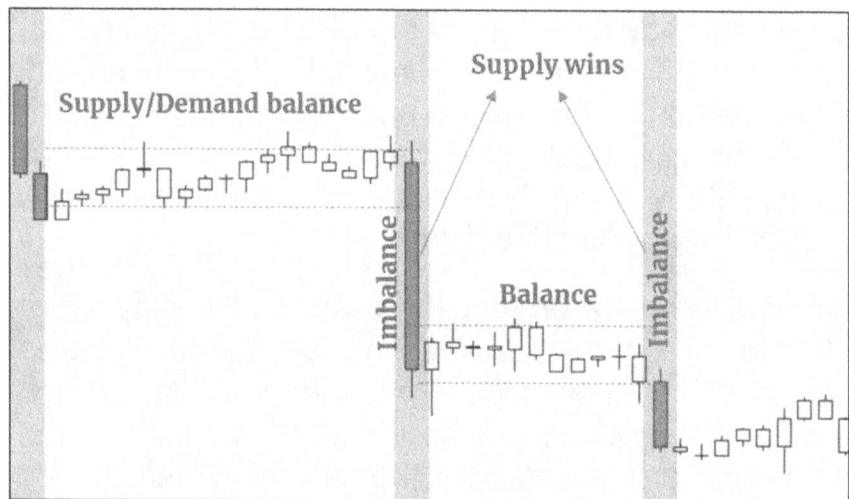

Figure 56. Balance and imbalance of supply/demand

The above argument is one of the many explanations for the reaction of the price to the big candles described in the previous sections. Again, this is not the entire picture for the role of the big players in the market. However, the presence of unfilled orders at certain price levels is a plausible explanation which cannot be ignored.

More candle types: the approach matters

In this section, you will learn about another aspect of the behavior of the market players which is very useful to understand. It will add another set of eyes to your analysis and help you to avoid placing the wrong limit orders. Figure 57 shows the same chart of the USDCAD used in the previous exercise. The only difference is that I have highlighted a different type of candle in order to train your eyes to see this particular aspect of how the market players behave.

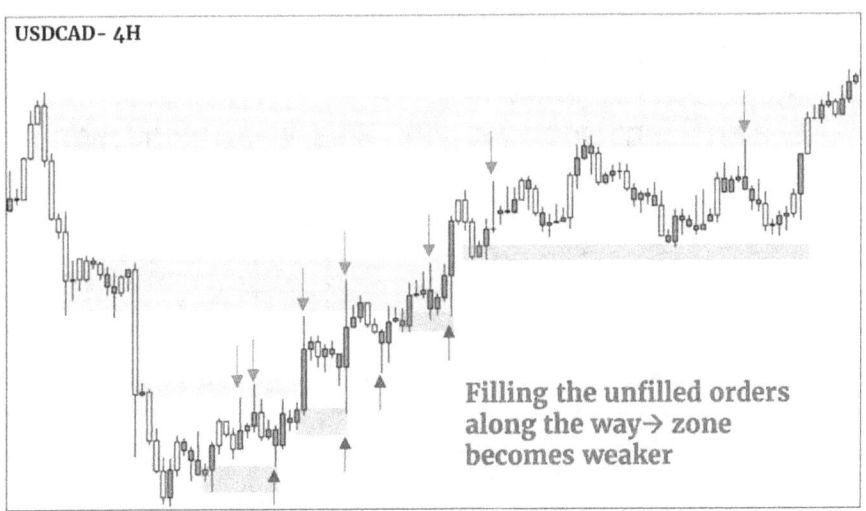

Figure 57. Elimination of the pending orders along the way

The gray candles on this chart (as opposed to the white candles) show the price behavior caused when the big players in the market remove the pending orders placed near each supply zone. What should you look for the first time such long tail candles occur? You need to determine whether that large amount of pending sell orders will cause another lower low (a term used to describe when the price moves to a new level lower than its previous low). In this case, each time the long tail candles shown by red downward arrows appear, the move down does not create a significant drop in the price. (If you are using the paper edition of this book rather than the e-book edition, the red colored arrows will obviously not present, but the seven arrows pointing downward of course do.) In fact, if you look at a lower time frame, you will probably see new demand zones being created along the way up. Some of these zones are shown as blue shaded areas on the chart. (Again, if you are using the paper edition, the blue shading will not appear, but you will see four darker gray rectangular areas primarily beside arrows pointing upward.) The gradual and steady upward movement in the price with the long tail consuming the pending orders is one way of approaching a supply or demand zone. In the last demand zone shown by the long and thin blue rectangle (dark gray in the paper edition of this book), it can be seen that the price was not able to breakdown even after reaching a significant supply zone. This is an indication of a true upward movement. Although several trades can be made using these zones in either direction, I normally look for the big moves. Nevertheless, understanding the behavior of each candle is important.

Let's look now at the chart in Figure 57 from a different point of view. The gradual upward movement zone has created multiple demand zones along its way. However, it is important to notice the appearance of long tail candles penetrating these zones as the price moves up. These are shown by the blue upward arrows on this chart. (As in the previous paragraph, if you are using the paper edition of this book rather than the e-book edition, the blue colored arrows will obviously not present, but the four arrows pointing upward of course do.) What does this tell you? It indicates that each time a demand zone (unfilled buy orders) is created, the buy orders are quickly consumed by the sellers, as indicated by these long tail candles. This means that if the price reaches a major supply zone, the move downward will be almost like a "free fall" as there are not many buy orders left on the way down. However, as mentioned earlier, this will occur only if some of these demand zones were broken by the sellers. This method of analyzing the price action in supply and demand trading is quite useful and important. Figures 58 and 59 show examples of how the approaching move to either the supply or demand zone can predict a potential big move in the future.

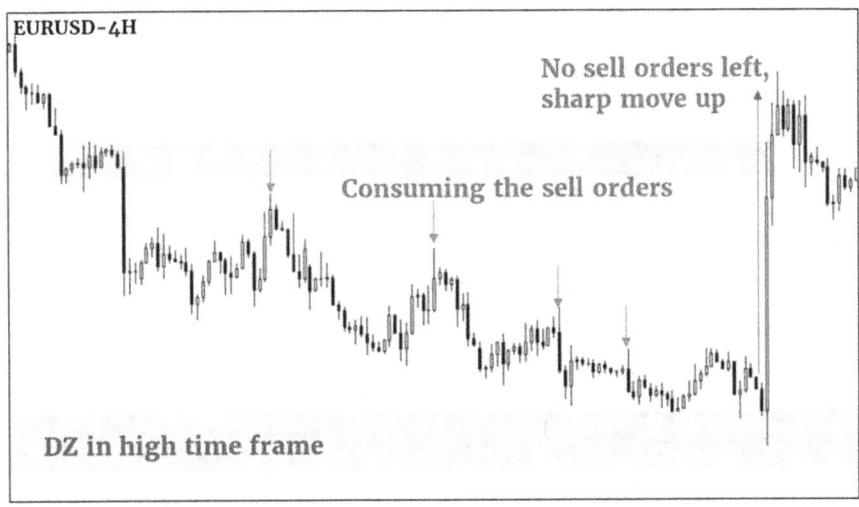

Figure 58. Consumption of the unfilled orders (you'll recall that DZ stands for demand zone)

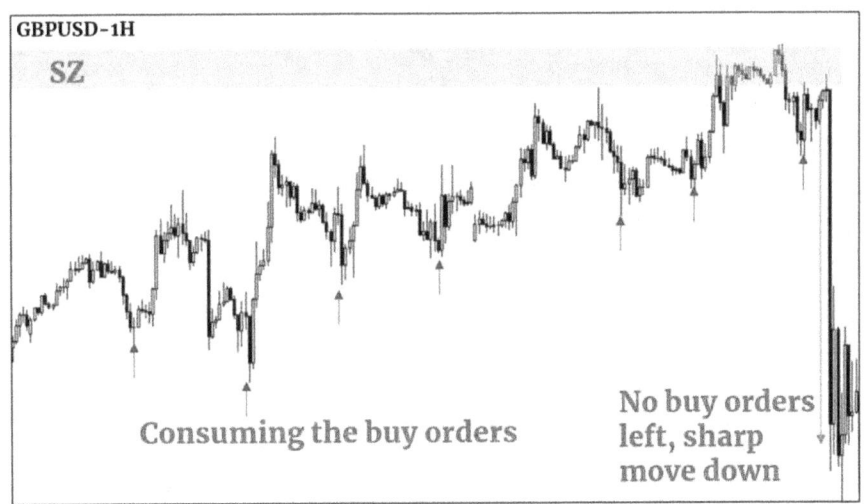

Figure 59. Reaction to the SZ with no pending orders left (you'll recall that SZ stands for supply zone)

Both examples show sharp moves away from a zone due to the lack of any pending buy or sell orders being in their way. The spikes in the price marked by arrows on both charts show the elimination of the pending orders. This process results in a clear path and thus a sharp movement in the price. If pending buy or sell orders were in the way, then the price movement would stall a bit.

Let's look a bit further into the psychology of the big players to help clarify why these types of patterns occur in the market. When you are thinking about these big players, you should consider the fact that they must execute a large number of profitable trades at any given time. Let's assume that a bank has decided to place their sell orders in the supply area shown in Figure 60. The big order has created a sharp drop in the price, and the bank has most likely taken some profit at the bottom of this sharp movement. In order for the banker to **sell** more or to fill their and the other banks' orders left at the supply, they have to create a large number of **buy** orders.

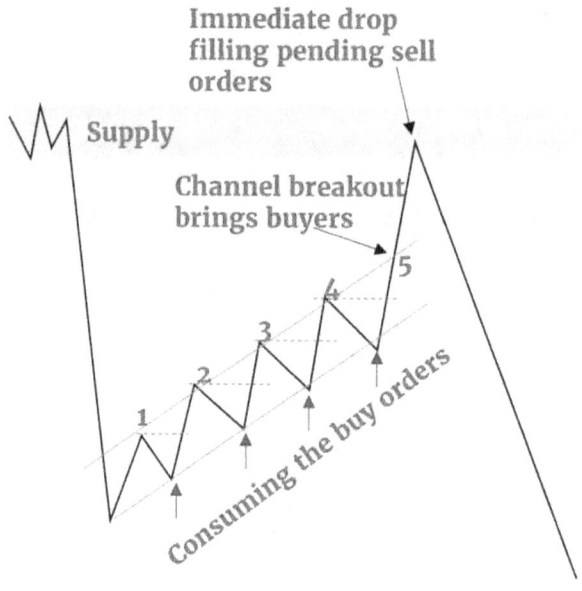

Figure 60. Psychology of the big players when selling large orders

The process that the big players have to go through to create a large number of buy orders is also illustrated in Figure 60. The first time the big players take some profit from their trades, they will be placing buy orders in the market to create the first upward move to point 1 on the schematic. By selling more, they will create a higher low on the chart. This will encourage some traders to buy in the hope of creating a higher high. Once the price breaks out of level 1, more buyers will step into the market and then a few sell orders will drop the price down to create another higher low. At this point, all of the trendline traders and channel traders can draw the channel lines on their charts. The break of each high and the creation of higher highs and higher lows will have many traders convinced that the trend is up. During this time, many supply and demand traders will also be involved, based on the lower time frame picture. The last set of buyers will come into the market when the price breaks out of the channel. This is a very bullish sign and many buy orders will now be in the market. This is what the big players need to execute their sell orders. (You will recall that "higher high" is a term used to describe when the price moves to a new level higher than its previous high, and "higher low" is a term used to describe when the price moves downward to a low level which is still higher than the previous lower price level.)

A few scenarios can occur, depending on the types of orders. The price will immediately drop if the orders are pending sell orders. On the other hand, the big players can wait for another set of stop loss orders from the breakout and the supply and demand traders who are now convinced that the trend is up. This will happen when the price is raised a bit higher outside of the supply zone and the buyers become convinced that the uptrend is real. In either case, the underlying market movers have taken out all of the barriers shown by the blue upward arrows in preparation for the next big drop. (Again, if you are using the paper edition of this book rather than the e-book edition, the blue colored arrows will obviously not present, but the arrows pointing upward in Figure 60 of course do.) In reality, more complex price action may very well occur, but a similar thought process will be involved. It is also worth noting that neither the gradual upward movement nor the sharp breakout has broken a higher time frame supply zone.

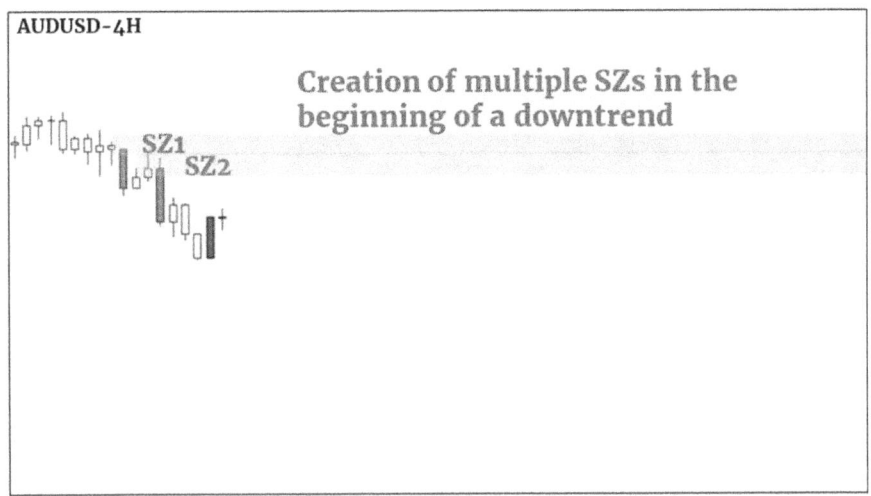

Figure 61. Real-time 4H chart of AUDUSD at the beginning of a downtrend (for your reference, SZ1 stands for supply zone 1 and SZ2 stands for supply zone 2)

Let's examine another real-time example that shows why the behavior of the price when *approaching* a zone is important. In this example, I will explain the evolution of the big player mindset from bearish to bullish for the AUDUSD pair at the beginning of the year 2013. Figures 61 and 62 show the 4H chart of this pair prior to the end of the year 2012.

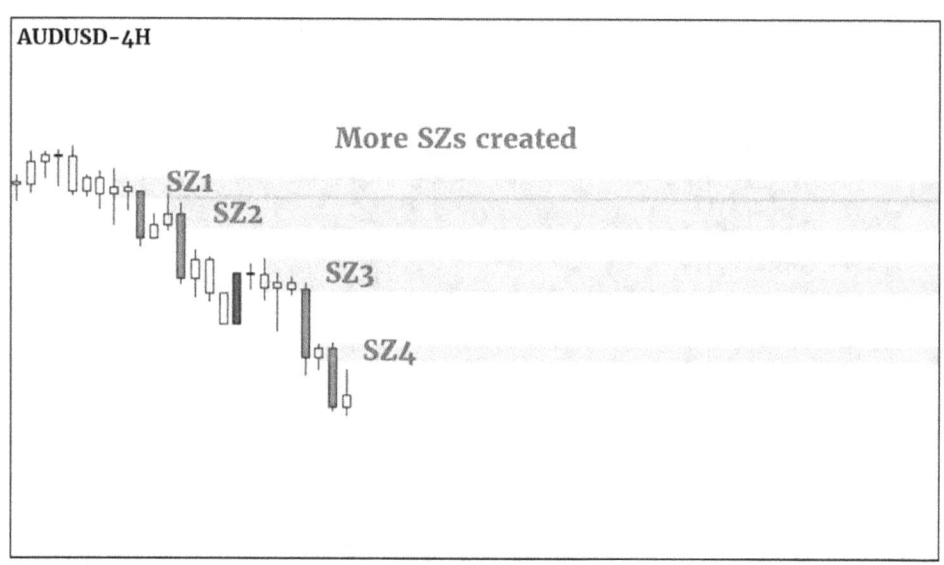

Figure 62. Real-time 4H chart of AUDUSD showing more SZs being created

As can be seen, a downtrend has already started with the creation of multiple supply zones on the way down. It is important to notice that SZ2 has penetrated into SZ1 before the continuation of the fall in price.

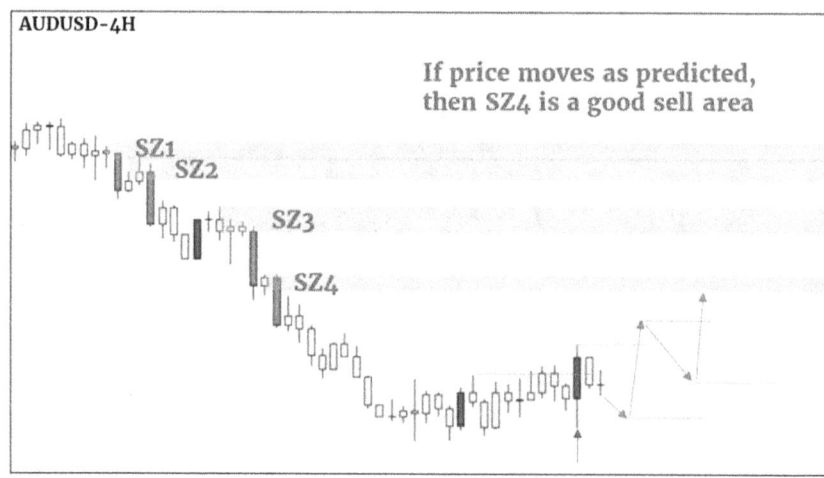

Figure 63. Creation of more SZs and the start of an approach back to the SZs

As Figure 63 illustrates, the price has created multiple supply zones on its way down. The downward movement though seems to have come to an end, or at least to have stalled. The price now has made a new high that is higher than the prior high level. At this point, you can anticipate a gradual movement toward the supply zones above to take advantage of the pending orders. The arrows on this chart show my prediction for the price movement to reach to the first immediate supply zone. Please notice that I have not yet opened any trades. For the time being, I am only watching the price movement to examine how it approaches the first supply zone. If the price moves in the way I anticipate, I can open sell orders near SZ4 with the prediction that the price will easily fall further down because of the removal of the demand zones along the way up.

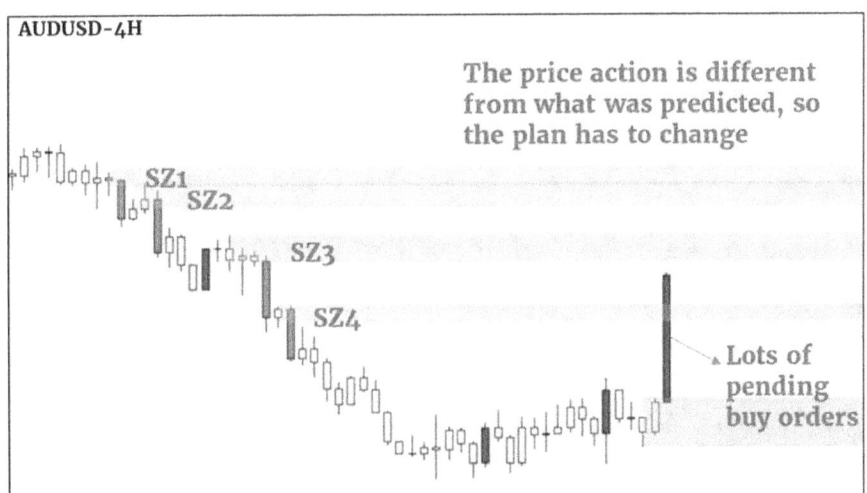

Figure 64. The removal of the SZ with a strong move upward

The dynamic of price action changes when there is a strong move up as seen in Figure 64. As the chart shows, SZ4 is removed within the price range of a single candle. By definition, such a strong candle indicates the creation of a new demand zone as shown in the green shaded area in Figure 64. (If you are using the paper edition of this book rather than the e-book edition, the green shading will obviously not present. The demand zone created is the rectangular shaded area near the bottom right-hand side of Figure 64.) You can anticipate the presence of many pending buy orders along the range of this candle. As the price has not approached SZ4 in the way expected, no sell orders have been opened at this point. Furthermore, such a strong movement toward the supply zones leads me to re-evaluate SZ3 for the placement of any sell orders. For the time being, I will place a pending short order near SZ1 where there seems to be some probability of price reaction. More importantly, the newly created demand zone is where I will place my buy order due to its strength in removing a supply zone.

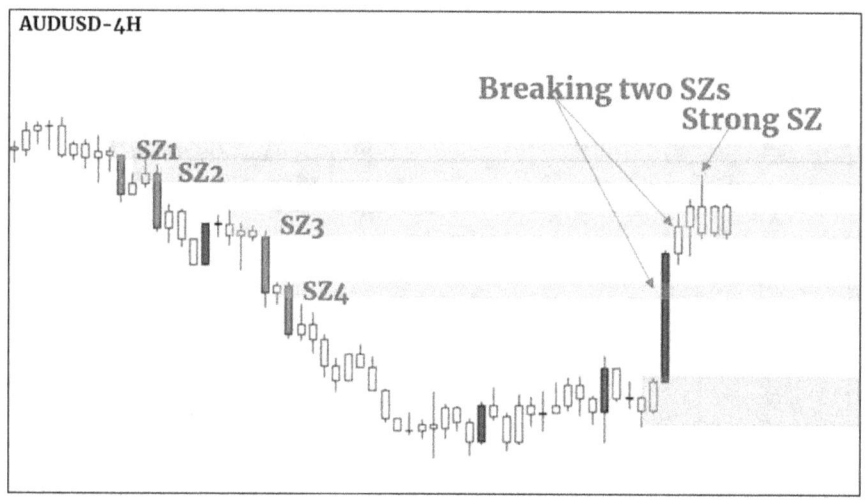

Figure 65. Removal of two SZs, thus adding to the DZ strength

Further movement in the price indeed confirms the strength of the demand zone, as shown in Figure 65. It adds to my confidence in placing the buy orders near this zone in the shaded area near the bottom of the big bullish candle (in the bottom right-hand corner of the figure). Also, you will have noticed that SZ2 seems to be a strong zone with numerous unfilled sell orders. The spike in the price near SZ2 is an indication of its strength. At this point, I know that I am in the middle of a battle between two strong zones (the demand zone vs. SZ2). Please note that SZ1 has not been affected and is therefore a good place to sell toward the demand zone. If I am not mistaken, the time period covered by this figure is near the release of the US non-farm payroll report (known as the NFP) in early January 2013. Strong movement was expected during that time. However, regardless of the news outcome, SZ1 and SZ2 are where you should place your sell orders.

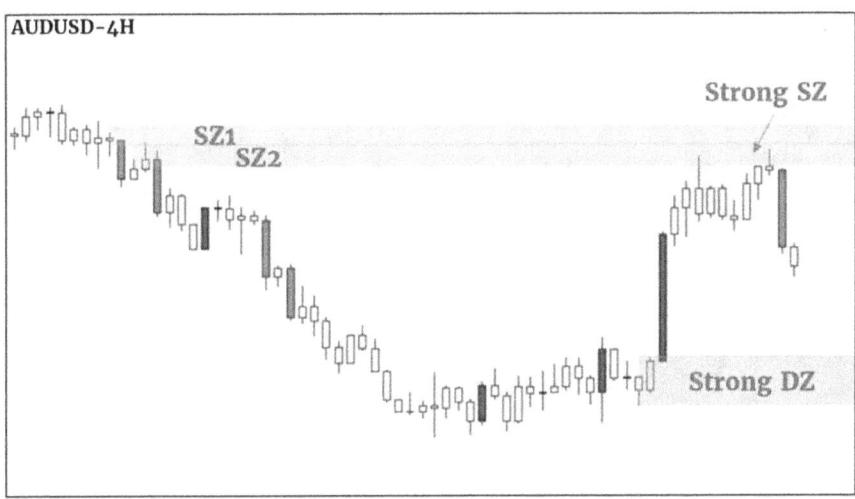

Figure 66. A strong move down provides confirmation of the strength of the SZs

As Figure 66 suggests, SZ1 and SZ2 are indeed strong. Any sell order in these zones would have been rewarded with considerable profit. Please note that SZ3 and SZ4 are removed from this chart since their significance has dropped to nothing. The strong drop in the price coincided with the good NFP report (the US non-farm payroll report mentioned in the previous paragraph). The main difference between this chart and the charts shown at the beginning of this section is the way the price approaches the supply zone. You cannot ignore the volume of unfilled buy orders during the creation of the demand zone. Therefore, any price movement toward this area is accompanied by the filling of many buy orders. This is why the first touch for such an important demand zone is crucial. Another important factor is the number of times that SZ2, and perhaps SZ1, have been touched compared to the demand zone on this chart. At the time of Figure 66, SZ2 has been touched twice and SZ1 has been touched once. The demand zone in this picture has not been touched even once. Based on this information, I anticipate that there must be a large number of pending buy orders near this level.

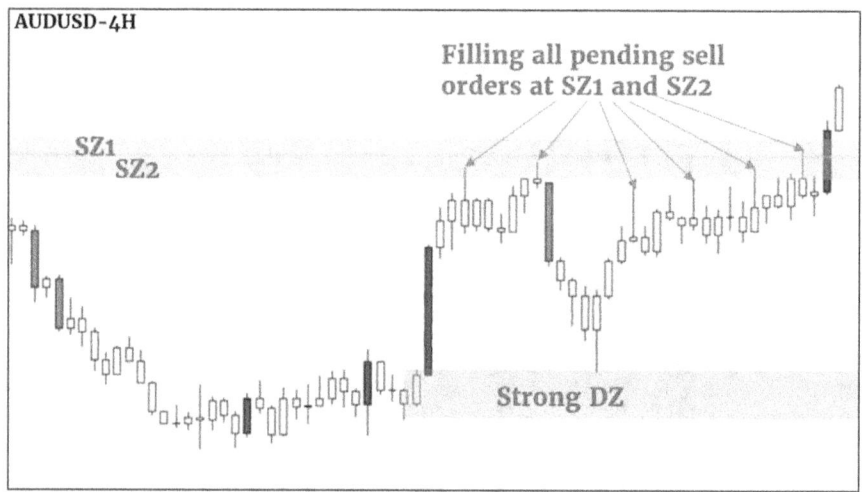

Figure 67. The first touch of the new DZ and filling the sell orders at SZ1 and SZ2

Figure 67 summarizes the importance of the first touch for the demand zone and the continuous consumption of the pending sell orders at SZ1 and SZ2. In many cases, traders, including myself, place their buy orders at the middle of the demand zone in order to reduce their risk. However, it is very important to realize the strength of the first touch. Moreover, the strength of SZ1 and SZ2 is evident in the number of price spikes into these two zones before they get removed.

The above example is a demonstration of the importance of approach. You need to evaluate the behavior of the big players and actually think like them when the price pushes near a prior supply zone or a prior demand zone. By now, you have probably realized that supply and demand trading does not mean only looking at large body candles. I suggest that you start looking at your charts and trying to think as if you are a big institutional trader. Try to imagine where you would be placing your buy and sell orders to maximize your profit. Consider how you can execute your large orders without having to sacrifice profit. In the following sections, I will touch on the basics of time frames and risk/reward analysis in supply and demand trading.

Should you care about different time frames?

It is essential to understand the importance of time frames when conducting supply and demand analysis. By intuition, you do not want to enter a short trade near a demand zone nor a long trade near a supply zone. However, when looking at a chart of a specific time frame, you could make a decision that is contradictory to the prediction of another time frame. For instance, you could be entering a long trade based on the 1H chart while you are near a supply zone on the daily chart. Remember, a supply zone is where there are many pending sell orders or where the big players add to their short trades.

Figure 68 shows an example of a demand zone that is created on the 4H chart of the NZDUSD pair due to the removal of the supply zone. As suggested by the chart, the demand zone is created by the break of the supply zone after multiple events of touching and penetration into the supply zone. However, the demand zone seems to have been easily removed by a single candle right after it was formed. This is what I call a "false" demand zone, which is the result of basing the analysis only on a single time frame chart.

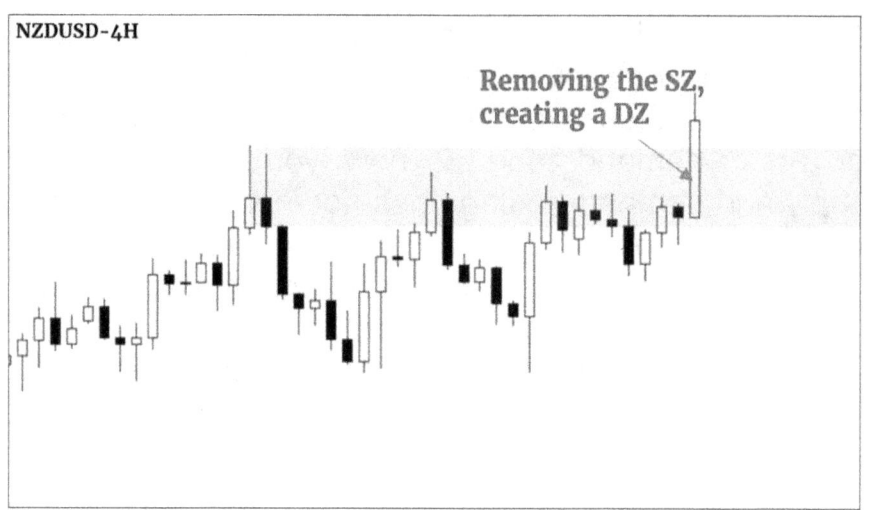

NZDUSD-4H

Removing the SZ, creating a DZ

NZDUSD-4H

DZ

Figure 68. Example of a false DZ

Figure 69 shows the same NZDUSD chart in both daily and 4H time frames. As the daily chart shows, the supply zone evidently is stronger than the newly created demand zone based on the 4H chart. Placing a buy order almost at the bottom of the supply zone does not seem to be the best trade idea after all.

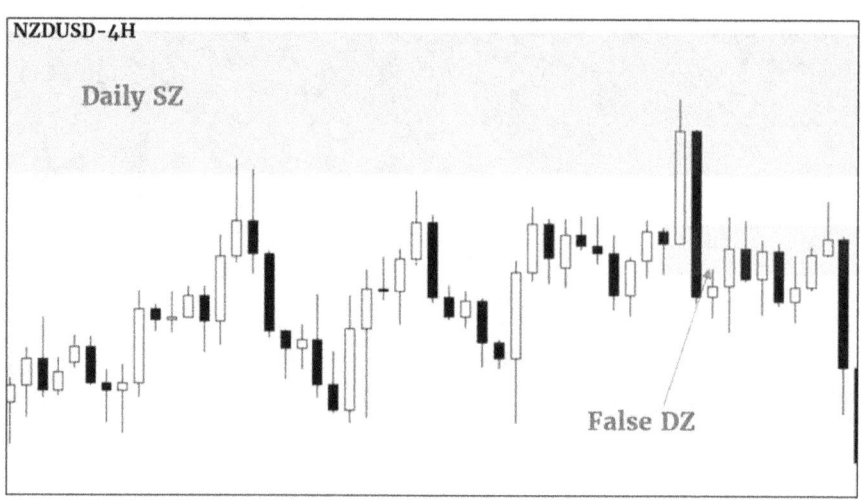

Figure 69. Importance of the time frame to determine supply and demand

Generally speaking, you need to examine the supply and demand in the perspective of at least two time frames. Usually the higher time frame determines the location of supply and demand zones, while the lower time frame provides a better entry point. An analogy to this is the two standard adjustment knobs, coarse and fine, on a microscope. The coarse knob focuses the lens in the right general direction, while the fine knob helps sharpen the image to the best quality possible.

In my experience, having two or three adjustment knobs, i.e., time frames, helps both to obtain a clearer picture of the price action and to better determine the right entry point. While the two high time frames clarify the direction of the trade, the third one should be used for choosing the right entry point. This concept will become even more important when determining the risk and reward for any trade. In most cases, I use the daily and 4H charts for determining the supply and demand zones, and I use the 1H chart for picking a good entry point. This selection of time frames mostly suits people seeking day-long or multi-day-long trades. For position traders, i.e., those who hold on and accumulate their position over a few days or even weeks, this sequence could go from monthly to weekly to daily charts. For short-term trading, i.e., day trading, the 4H chart is the highest time frame while 1H and 15M charts are used for identifying the direction of your trade and fine-tuning your entry point. In the case of day trading, the spread is a vital factor to pay attention to. I use the day trading time sequence for the major pairs where the spread is minimal. A high spread could easily span through at least 50% of the overall range of a zone and very likely reach to your stop loss before going in your expected direction.

Where is the zone?

As discussed on the charts shown in the beginning of this section, the main characteristic of a supply or demand zone is the appearance of large body candles. I would like to emphasize that these zones are simply the consequence of the underlying imbalance between the short and long trades placed by the big institutional traders. Wherever you see these large body candles, be certain that you mark them on your chart. This approach of looking at the charts and understanding the mindset of the big players takes patience and practice in order to become intuitive. My suggestion is to allow your brain to take its course and develop a natural identification algorithm for this style of trading.

In many cases, you may find it easier to start with a mechanical method of identifying the zones. This section describes some well-known patterns among traders to identify these zones. While these patterns are definitely helpful in finding the right zones, please bear in mind that the proper signal lies within the behavior of each price bar. In essence, each and every single candle or bar matters. Although the mechanical way of marking a supply or demand zone on the chart works most of the time, the understanding of what happened during the lifetime of each price bar is what makes the difference. In the following paragraphs, I will explain the major types of patterns commonly used by traders to mark these zones. I will then show another set of almost similar patterns and explain how the same pattern could lead you to draw the wrong zones.

The four major types of **price action patterns** that are used by supply and demand traders are as follows:

Rally-Base-Drop (abbreviated as RBD): this pattern occurs when a rally in the price (the price is increasing in an upward direction) stalls and the price then drops in the opposite direction. Figure 70 demonstrates an example of this pattern on a candlestick chart.

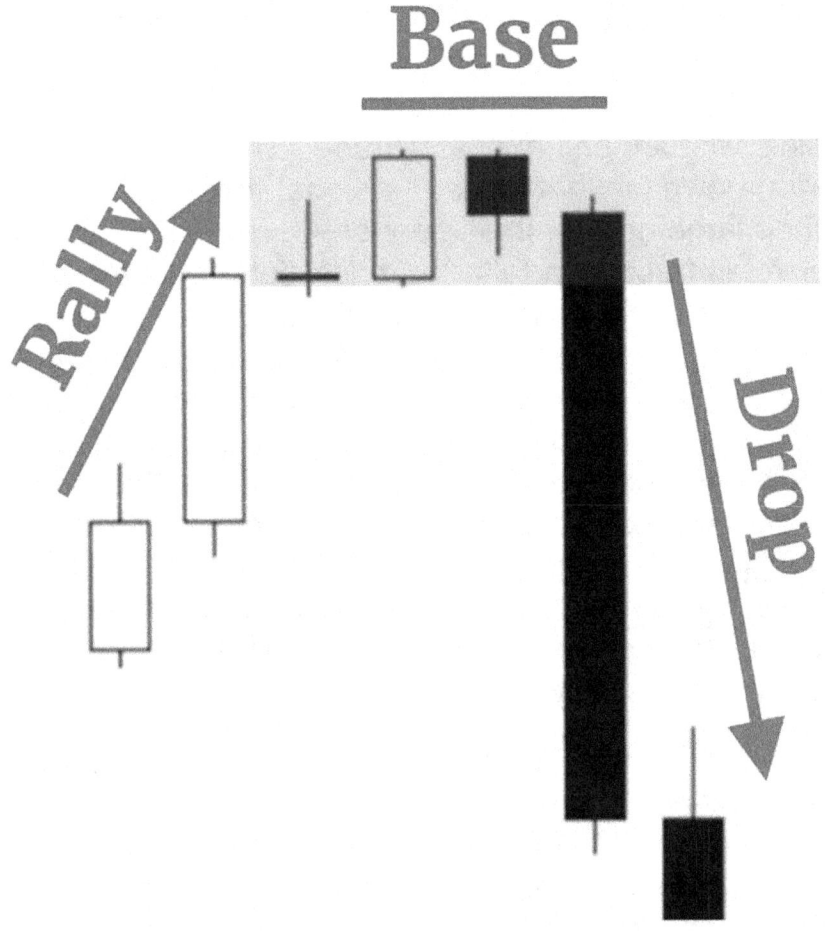

Figure 70. RBD pattern creates an SZ

It is important to think about what occurred during the course of these few candles. A strong move in the upward direction stopped at a certain level. Prior to this level (base), the bullish traders were driving the price up with the hope of a continuous rally. Many retail traders probably joined the rally too late near the top and now the price has stalled. It seems that the base is where the buyers and sellers have come to a temporary agreement in the price, and an equilibrium is in place. A movement in any direction is met with orders in the opposite direction and hence, a range without direction is created. Please notice that in this time period (where the base is), you would have almost no clue as to where the price will be for the next candle. Accordingly, you should only watch the price action from outside without entering any trade. The strong move (large body candle) down is what gives the signal that the big players are entering their large orders. It is important to remember that it is very difficult for retail traders to take the price outside of the equilibrium range. A fundamental change or continuation of such a change drives the big bankers to take the price outside of the equilibrium zone. Many large sell orders must have been placed to create such a strong drop. It is very likely that many of their orders have not been filled. If one set of bankers has decided that the price should fall, others will come to a similar conclusion sooner or later, and they all will have to find buyers. The result is that an overflow of sell orders will be present on the market and they will have to be filled. An institutional trader would not want to sell at the bottom of that large drop candle; I hope you agree with me on that.

Before such a drop, you will have no indication of what these big players are thinking. Now you do have a hint and you will mark up your chart based on that hint. The shaded area around the base is where you draw your supply zone. The opinions among seasoned traders differ regarding how big the range should be and where to choose the bottom and top of the zone. Many would consider that the bottom of the zone should coincide with the body of candles in the base and the top should be the maximum price in the range. Some only consider the bodies of candles and not the wicks. Regardless, the important concept here is that you realize the level at which the big players were comfortable selling the instrument. Very often, you will see that the price comes very close to but never quite reaches that supply zone, and then it will drop again. Why? Because you do not have the capability to see all of those sell orders along the range of the big body drop candle. You must make your decision based on probability principles. You predict that the probability of having unfilled pending orders is the highest within that supply zone. It does not mean though that there are no pending orders outside of that range in the lower prices. In fact, depending on the amount of risk you are willing to take, you can enter a trade at a lower price than the supply zone, as long as you know the zone is strong.

How do you know that a zone is strong? The strength of a zone depends on where it originates. A move to come out of a long-term trend is much stronger than a continuation of a trend. It takes a considerable number of orders to turn a downtrend into an uptrend. In order to be considered a zone, an area where the price stalls must first have removed its prior opposite side zones (the opposite of a demand zone is a supply zone, and vice versa). Thus, for a demand zone to become strong, it must have removed at least one supply zone preceding that demand zone. The more zones it removes, the stronger it becomes. Again, it takes a large number of orders to remove multiple zones of the opposite side.

Drop-Base-Rally (abbreviated as DBR): a pattern that happens when a strong downward movement stalls but is then followed by a strong move in the upward direction. This pattern creates a demand zone. Figure 71 shows an example of such a pattern on a candlestick chart.

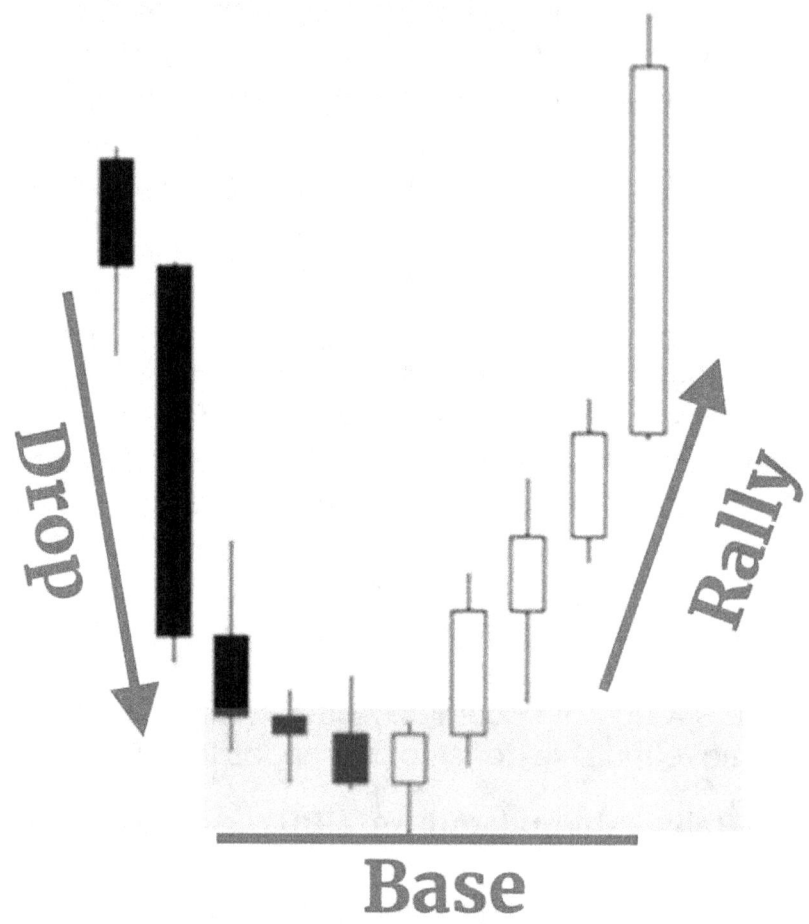

Figure 71. DBR pattern creates a DZ

Again, you should look for strong large body candles exiting an equilibrium range. Once you see such a pattern, you should mark up your chart in the base area as a demand zone.

Rally-Base-Rally (abbreviated as RBR): this is a type of continuation pattern, meaning that a rally in the price stalls, but is then followed by further buying, judged by a big move out of the stalling zone in the same rally direction. Depending on the time frame, two types of this pattern could appear on your charts. Figure 72 shows these two variations of the Rally-Base-Rally pattern.

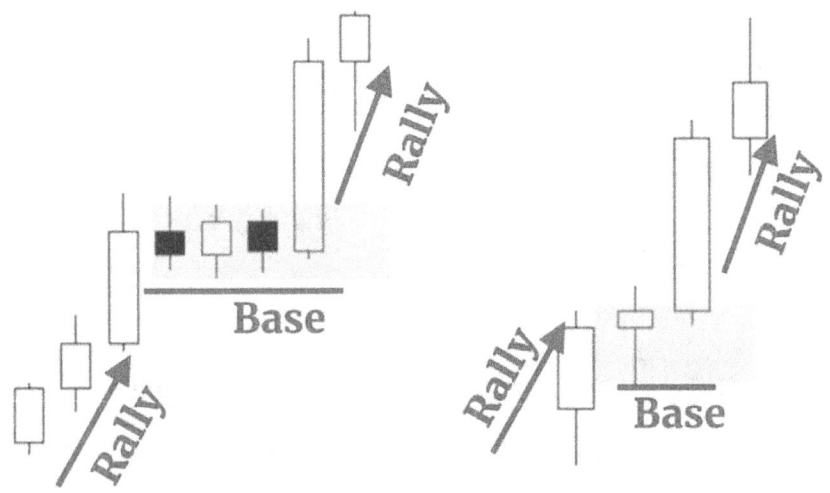

Figure 72. RBR pattern creates a DZ

In both scenarios, the price shows a sharp upward movement that is followed by another sharp move after a temporary stall. In many cases, it is this type of pattern that results in the removal of a prior strong supply zone. When a Rally-Base-Rally removes a prior supply zone, the base area becomes a strong demand zone. By definition, the previous Drop-Base-Rally also becomes a strong demand zone. An example of this is illustrated in Figure 73.

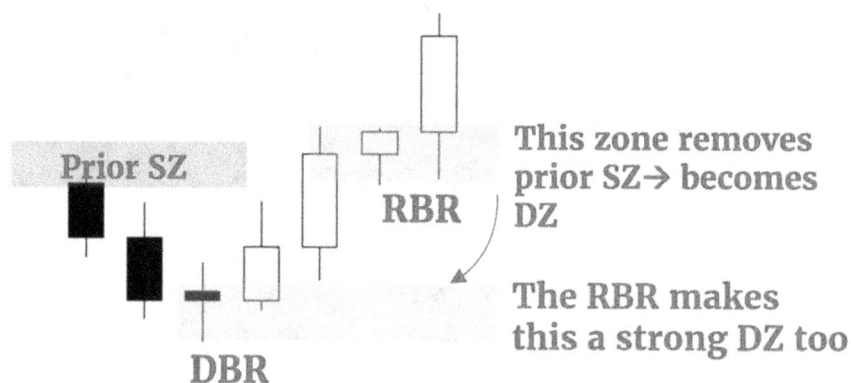

Figure 73. RBR removes supply, makes the DBR a strong DZ

Drop-Base-Drop (abbreviated as DBD): this is another continuation pattern, in which a sharp drop in the price stalls and is then followed by another sharp drop from the temporary equilibrium zone. This type of pattern creates a supply zone. Quite often, the Drop-Base-Drop is responsible for removing a prior demand zone. Similar to the scenario in Figure 73, the Drop-Base-Drop, as it removes a demand zone, makes the immediate previous Rally-Base-Drop a strong supply zone. The two variations of the Drop-Base-Drop pattern are shown in Figure 74. As with the previous case for the Rally-Base-Rally, the base consists of a few ranging candles or a bullish candle that has a smaller body and range size compared to its neighboring large body candles. (The term "ranging candles" refers to a series of candles where the price does not show a direction and only fluctuates inside of a range.)

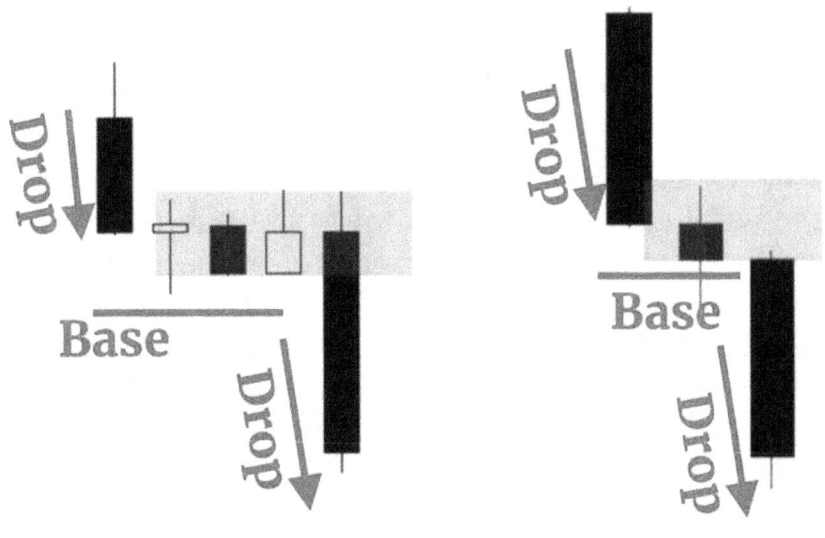

Figure 74. DBD pattern creates an SZ

The above-mentioned four patterns are all comprised of typical price action: the price moves toward a level, then stalls at that level to create a temporary equilibrium zone, and then makes another move in the same or opposite direction of the initial movement. The sharp exit from the equilibrium zone is what makes it a supply or demand zone. How to draw the zone or where to place the top and bottom of the zone depends on personal preferences and the risk/reward ratio. (More about the risk/reward ratio will be presented in the following section.) The more important factor is that you realize the probability of existing pending orders around these levels and how you can use this probability to your advantage.

Before ending this section, let's examine a few cases where patterns similar to those described above appear on the chart but do not represent a high quality supply or demand zone. Figure 75 shows an example of what seems to be a Drop-Base-Rally creating a demand zone. In essence, it looks very similar to the example in Figure 71. However, please pay attention to the long tail of the first bullish candle at the start of the rally. What does that tell you? The fact that a drop has been stalled on a base level and was followed by a move up is truly a Drop-Base-Rally type of behavior. However, the appearance of the tail indicates that many buy orders have been consumed before the buyers took control of the price. This means that you cannot expect many leftover unfilled buy orders at this level the next time the price visits it. The lower the probability of unfilled orders, the lower your chances of picking a good buy entry in this case.

DBR

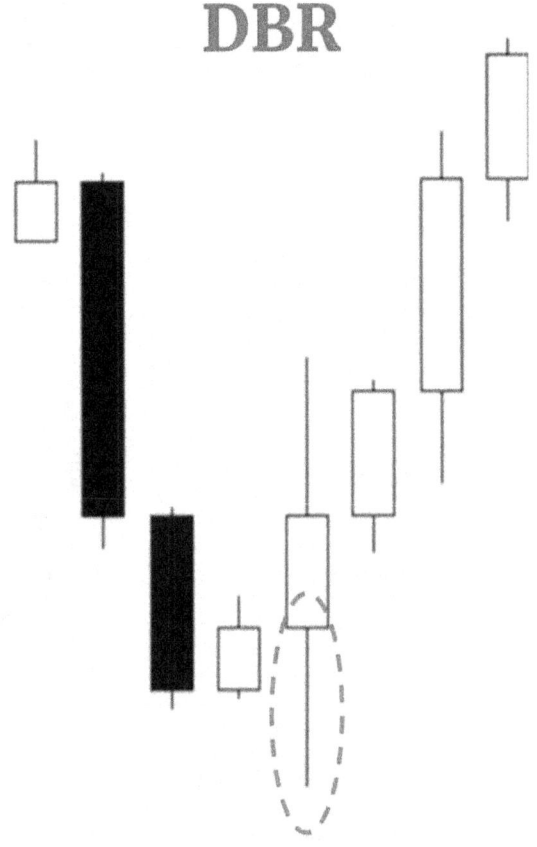

Figure 75. DBR does not create a DZ

Figure 76 shows an example of a Drop-Base-Drop appearing to create a supply zone. Would you be able to use the range on this chart as a supply zone? Why or why not?

Figure 76. DBD does not create an SZ

In this case, the area shown in the dashed box could be a potential supply zone. It satisfies the requirements of a supply zone based on a Drop-Base-Drop pattern: a sharp drop in the price stalls (creating an equilibrium range), and then, after some time passes, it leaves that zone in a sharp manner. So, why isn't this zone a good quality supply zone? Again, the reason lies in the underlying price action. Imagine this Figure 76 is a 4H chart (remember, on your 4H chart each candle represents a period of four hours). Please take a moment and count the candles in the "boxed in" area of this figure where the price has stalled. There's 12 intervals of time with each one representing four hours. The big players have therefore spent about 48 hours (two days) in this level before making their decision. Do you think there would be any unfilled orders left after this period of time? I would like to think not. The probability of having lots of pending orders or new big players entering the market at this level is very low. These players are those who did not find a good entry point to place their sell orders and are waiting for the price to reach back to this level. Do you think there is anyone left who would not have found enough time in these 48 hours to make their decision? Again, the chances are low, and for that reason I would not rely on the quality of this zone.

Figure 77 shows examples of the Drop-Base-Drop and Rally-Base-Rally continuation patterns. These patterns create, respectively, supply and demand zones. However, in each example, notice the tail of the first immediate candle after what seems to be a base. Those candle tails are encircled by dashed lines.

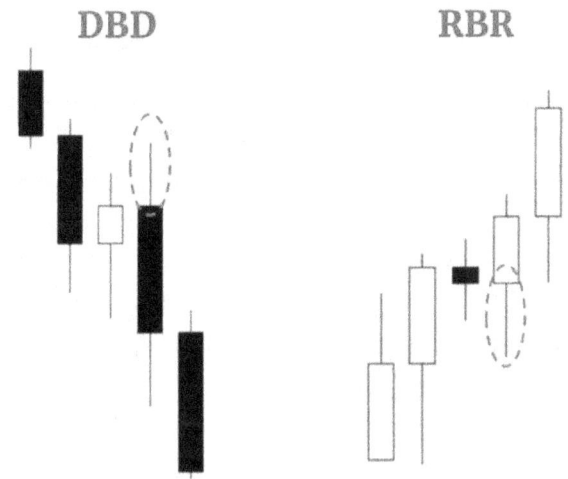

Figure 77. DBD and RBR do not create, respectively, an SZ and a DZ

In these two scenarios, the base candle is surrounded by neighboring large body candles, suggesting the possibility that the price will leave the zone before filling all orders. However, the tail penetration into and beyond the base candle range suggests otherwise. It seems that all of the leftover orders at this range have been already executed before the price leaves the zone. As a result, the probability of having any pending orders the next time the price reaches to this level has decreased significantly. This is the reason why understanding the behavior of the market players is more important than a pure mechanical determination of the supply and demand zones. It is quite possible to imagine numerous other scenarios where these patterns cannot predict a reliable zone. Many simultaneous factors are in play at any given time in the market, and it is impossible in any book to go over every single example. I hope I have been able to provide you with at least a basic understanding of the method of analysis that I use in my own trading. The next section describes the very critical part of trading: determining the entry and exit for any trade.

Risk/reward ratio: stop loss and target profit

Perhaps the most important part of planning for any trade is determining the amount of risk being taken in the anticipation of a reward. In almost any type of investment, this is often referred to as the risk/reward ratio. The right ratio to consider when planning for a trade mostly depends on your trading style, risk-taking appetite and preferred frequency of trading. If you are an aggressive trader, taking the risk/reward ratio of 1/1 could be your normal routine. Indeed, for the day trading style, it is difficult to find high reward trades within the time frame of a few hours. Regardless of the style, taking trades with a risk higher than the reward is not a sustainable methodology. In the long term, you will lose all of your money by taking higher risk trades.

One of the advantages of supply and demand trading over many other trading styles is the straightforward determination of risk and reward. In short, you do not want to be in a trade once all of the pending orders have been consumed. Also, you do not want to extend your trades beyond the level where all pending orders are outstanding. The former determines your risk, while the latter determines your target profit.

As mentioned, depending on the style and frequency of trading, the risk/reward ratio differs among traders. In my day trading, I often consider trades with a risk/reward ratio of 1/1, while for longer-term swing trades, a risk/reward ratio of at least 1/2 or 0.5 is what I look for to enter a trade. In addition to considering multiple time frames as you analyze the charts, risk is a key factor in determining whether to enter a trade or not. It will be more helpful for you if I go over some real examples of how to determine the risk/reward ratio rather than only provide several paragraphs of text.

Figure 78 shows a chart of USDJPY in the daily time frame. As you can see, I marked up three supply zones on this chart: a Rally-Base-Drop and two Drop-Base-Drop types of supply zones. SZ1, which is a Rally-Base-Drop, is not a high quality supply zone for the reasons I explained in the previous section. However, SZ2 and SZ3 have high quality because they have removed some demand zones in the past (not shown).

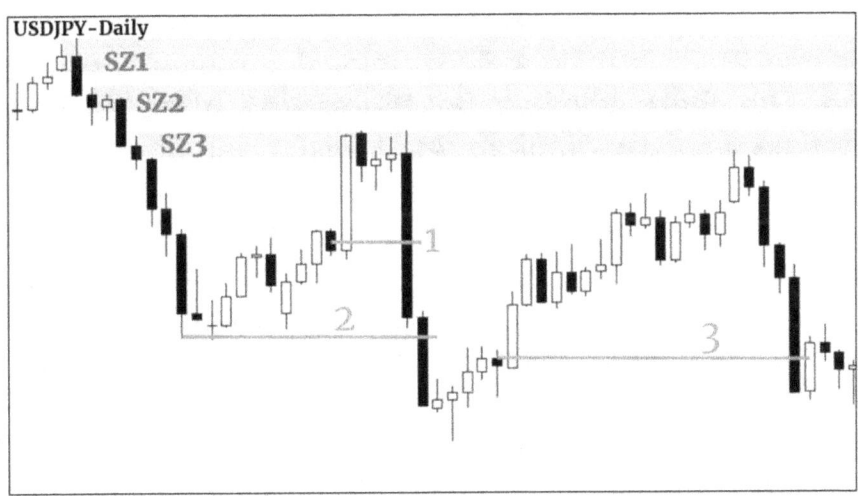

Figure 78. USDJPY daily chart with some SZs marked

Beside the zones, I also marked up three levels with green horizontal lines on this chart and numbered them 1, 2 and 3. (If you are using the paper edition of this book rather than the e-book edition, the green lines will obviously not present. The three levels are the lines numbered 1, 2 and 3 below the supply zones.) These lines indicate the first immediate price levels for taking profit in my short trades. Why? In brief, they correspond to the closest possible demand zones where I anticipate some pending buy orders are left. Based on my previous explanations, none of these lines truly describe a good quality demand zone. However, looking at the final picture after the completion of the chart is significantly different from real-time trading. At the time of entering the first short near SZ3, I would be certain that there are some unfilled buy orders near line 1. I would plan my trade in such a way that I exit half of the position at line 1 and then move my stop loss near the entry point or slightly into the profit area, also referred to as moving the stop loss to breakeven (BE). The next target profit would be near line 2, where I expect some more buy orders to enter into the market.

As you can see on the chart, the first drop from SZ3 has been able to remove two significant levels with some demand characteristics (lines 1 and 2). This makes SZ3 a significant level for future trade planning. The chart indicates that the approach toward SZ3 for the second time is very gradual. As I discussed in the "approach method" section, this type of behavior is accompanied by the removal of temporary demand zones along the way up to SZ3. However, I marked line 3 and my target profit for the second short trade from SZ3. This is due to the large body candle without much retracement from line 3, and this makes it a possible demand zone. Now that I have determined where I want to exit out of my trades, it is time to determine how much risk I am willing to absorb. The following discussion is my personal way of determining the risk and how I decide on the stop loss level. It could vary among traders, and

I recommend you create your own strategy based on my explanations.

Before continuing on with this example, I want to provide a "mini-refresher" lesson on what the unit of measurement known as a pip is, as the term hasn't been referenced since near the beginning of this book. A pip is the smallest number to represent the change in the value of the exchange rate for a pair. It is the last decimal point of a currency pair exchange rate. In most cases, the currency pairs are displayed down to four or five decimal points. The fourth decimal point is considered as the pip value. For instance, if USDCAD moves from 1.2132 to 1.2133, you would say the USD rises by one pip. The exceptions to this are the JPY pairs, which are displayed to only two decimal places, and the second decimal point defines the pip. In many cases, traders report their profit and loss in terms of pips, rather than in an actual dollar amount.

Returning now to the example, I set out the first scenario in Figure 79: a typical sell order with its corresponding stop loss (from this point forward abbreviated as SL) and target profit (from this point forward abbreviated as TP). As you study this example, don't forget that since this is a JPY pair, the currency pair exchange rate would only be displayed to two decimal places, with the second decimal place defining the pip.

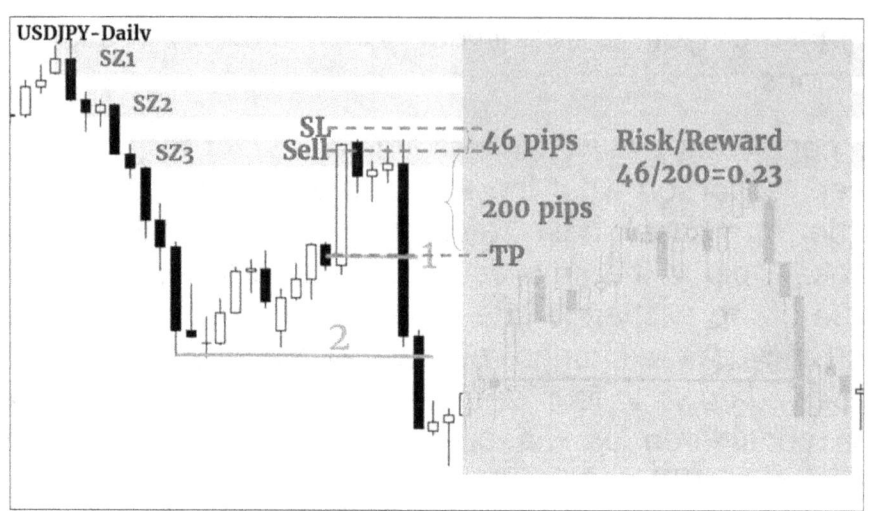

Figure 79. Determining SL and TP, risk/reward example

In this scenario, the sell order is placed at the middle of the supply zone. This is a reasonable place for entering a trade to minimize the amount of risk. The SL is placed a few pips above the top of the supply zone. In this case, it is almost 46 pips above the top border of SZ3. The first TP level is near line 1, as explained previously. The total number of pips between the TP and the sell order is 200, which results in a risk/reward ratio of 0.23 (46/200). This is a very safe and reasonable ratio. In most cases, I consider any values below 0.5 to be a sufficiently safe and reasonable enough ratio to enter a trade. This is illustrated in Figure 80.

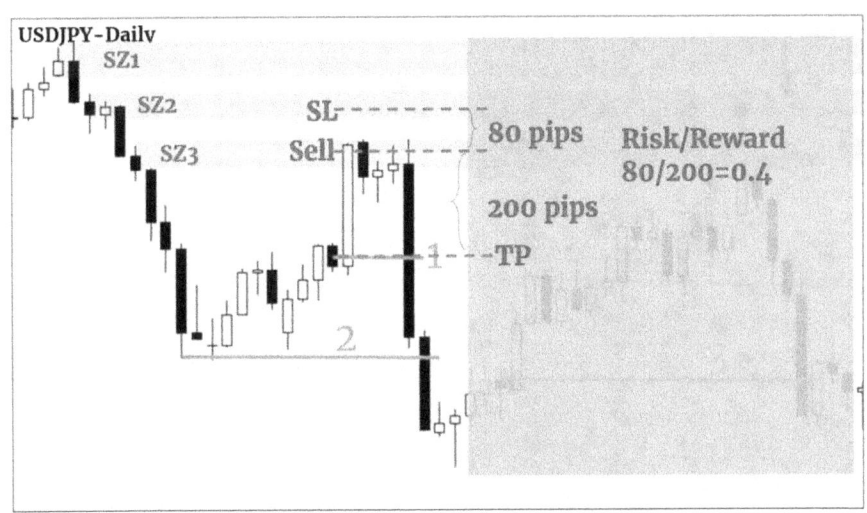

Figure 80. Example of extending the amount of risk

The choice of extending my risk to a higher level has a great significance. Placing my SL well above SZ3 and, in fact, into SZ2 ensures that many sell orders must be filled before my SL order is executed. In real-time trading, often the SL is reached before the TP is achieved. In Chapter 2, I described how brokers function and why they hunt for SL orders. For this particular case, I would still choose the first option explained in Figure 79. This is because of the way the price approaches SZ3 for the first time. The appearance of a large body candle suggests the activity of some big players, and this signals a need to minimize my risk.

For the second portion of the sell order in Figure 79, the TP is near line 2 and the SL is moved to the breakeven level. It is not wise to aim for line 2 as the only TP level while a zone near line 1 (where a strong upward move started) is present. Following the first reaction to SZ3, it is evident that this zone has a potential to be used as a selling point. This is based on the fact that SZ3 has removed two significant levels near lines 1 and 2. Figure 81 shows the example of a trade from the second touch of this zone.

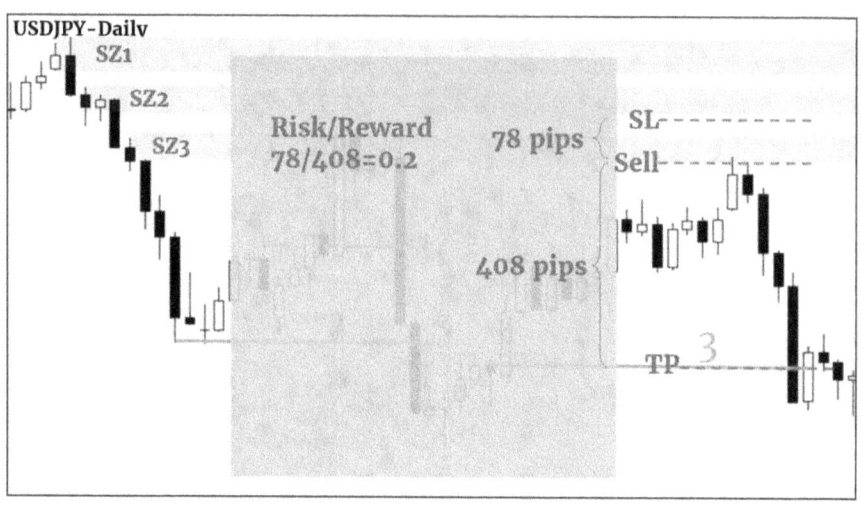

Figure 81. Examples of SL and TP for a sell order

In this scenario, the entry point is very close to the bottom border of SZ3. This is due to the creation of a new supply zone from the first touch of SZ3. The large body drop candle created a new supply zone with a bottom border lower than the original SZ3 (not shown here). Nevertheless, it is very normal to miss the chance of entering a trade due to a difference of a few pips. Because of the potential of reaching good profits based on the TP, it is safe to enter the trade at the bottom border of SZ3 and therefore not miss the entry opportunity. As can be seen in Figure 81, the risk/reward ratio of 0.2 is very low, and that makes it a very profitable trade. Again, please notice that all of these discussions are based on a chart from the past and, in reality, nothing is that easy. However, the thought process of determining the risk and reward remains intact. As a trader, you should always plan for a trade and predetermine your exit strategy. The plan should not change during a trade.

However, it will often happen that your initial analysis that you based your plan on is faulty. In those cases, you will see the trade moving against your expectation, making you realize your mistake in the analysis stage. This has happened to me numerous times and it will happen to you. In fact, all of the price action tips and tricks I described in the previous section, the candle-by-candle behavior analysis, and the careful evaluation of the supply and demand zones in multiple time frames are the results of my mistakes and learning process during real-time trading. My goal here is to pass on my experiences and lessons from these mistakes to you. However, always be prepared for new behavior in the market, for new tricks being played by the big market players, and ultimately for the need to modify your strategy.

As a conclusion to this book, the next chapter is dedicated to a series of real-time chart analyses and trades I have taken in the past. This is a compilation of my successes and failures in my journey to master supply and demand trading. It will be beneficial to read, understand and practice the content of this current chapter before proceeding to the concluding chapter. You will find the source of the lessons in this upcoming chapter to be mistakes I have made in the past. After all, forex trading is a never-ending learning process that requires your constant focus and attention - all of the time. Fortunately, practice makes perfect. As I always say, do not rely on back-testing these strategies. Instead, forward test. Make your best effort to overcome the initial steep learning curve and do not let your failures frustrate you. Your brain will take care of the rest.

CHAPTER 3: TRADING JOURNAL

An educational account of successful and failed trades

I n this chapter, I will present a series of my past pre-trade analyses, thought processes and planning. This is a very small sampling of my trading activity, but I believe these examples will serve as useful educational materials. These real-time trade planning and execution processes are intended to supplement the materials in the previous chapter. Each example is titled by the initial date I started the trade planning. I structured each example by going through a sequence of time frame variations in order for you to see how I determined my entry, SL and TP. I recommend that you pay special attention to my thought process and why the trade worked or did not work. Moreover, I will pose thought-provoking questions (marked by "**Q**") along the way and ask you to think about and answer those questions before moving forward. My aim is to provide as much forward testing experience as possible before you enter the live forex world. So, let's begin.

USDJPY- Jan. 30, 2017

Duration: **medium term** | Time frames: **1D-8H-4H** | Profit/Loss=**395 pips**

Figure 82 shows the daily chart of the USDJPY on Monday, January 30th, 2017. You will see that the pair opened that morning with a gap down.

Figure 82. USDJPY 1D chart on Jan. 30, 2017

Q1: Can you mark up the possible supply and demand zones on this chart?

Q2: What is the current trend of the market?

Figure 83 shows the most immediate and useful-to-me nearby zones on the chart. As can be seen on this chart, the overall trend of the pair seems to be down. Why? Look at the far-left side of the chart where demand zones have been created. The current dominant trend seems to be removing every prior demand zone one after the other. On the other hand, the newly created supply zones are not being violated, i.e., the price shows strong reaction to each supply zone once it reaches them. The daily chart in this scenario is my bigger time frame to determine the overall sentiment of the market on this pair.

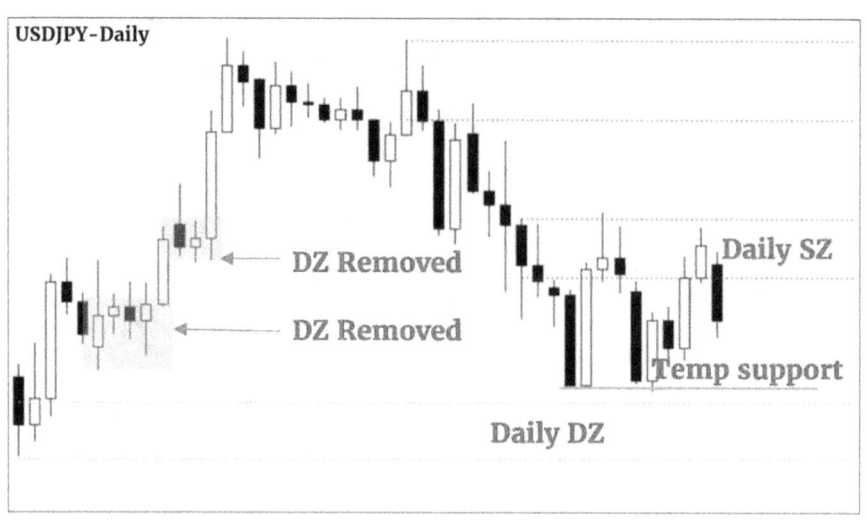

Figure 83. Daily chart tracking market sentiment along with my marking of SZs and DZs

The two most immediate supply and demand zones are marked on this chart by the small dashed lines. Another supply zone near the top right-hand side of the chart is also marked, but that is irrelevant to my current decision-making.

Q3: Why is what I have marked as the daily supply zone in fact a supply zone? What is the quality of this supply zone?

The two major reasons for marking this as the daily supply zone are as follows:

- The price has shown significant sharp downward reaction from that zone.

- The zone is responsible for removing a demand zone.

The quality of this zone is not good. There has been at least one attempt toward breaking this zone, and there are minimal chances of there being many leftover sell orders around this zone. However, for the moment I am only looking at this zone as a potential supply zone. In fact, I am anticipating the break of the temporary support level, shown as the solid line on the bottom right-hand side of this chart, and the price reaching to the daily demand zone, shown by the dashed line. Why am I not thinking of buying on the touch of this demand zone? It is because the trend is down and I am more biased toward selling. It should take at least a few days for me to develop a better picture of this trade idea. Figure 84 shows the same chart after 10 trading days. As expected, the daily demand zone has shown some strength and now the price is approaching the daily supply zone.

Figure 84. Same USDJPY daily chart after 10 days

At this time, it is appropriate to look at the lower time frames and fine-tune the entry decision. The medium time frame (8H in this case) helps me to confirm the trend and examine the strength of the supply and demand zones.

Figure 85. USDJPY 8H chart used to confirm the trend (the meaning of LL and LH are explained below)

As Figure 85, the 8H chart, suggests, the price is making lower highs (marked as LH in this figure, "lower high" is a term used to describe when the price moves to a new level lower than its previous high) and lower lows (marked as LL in this figure, "lower low" is a term used to describe when the price moves to a new level lower than its previous low) as it is removing the prior demand zones. None of the demand zones have been able to remove the newly created supply zones and hence, the trend is still down.

The time frame that I use for making the trade decision and execution is the 4H chart. Figure 86 is the price action prior to the arrival of the price to the daily supply zone.

Figure 86. USDJPY 4H chart used for decision-making

On this chart, I show the most recent candle as it approaches the daily supply zone. I also marked the presence of a gap near the top of the daily supply zone. A gap is similar to a supply zone in the sense that there may be some unfilled orders in the gap region. Before discussing the most important candle, candle 4, let's examine the preceding candles. The way these candles approach the supply zone shows an initial departure from the daily demand zone followed by a gradual move up. The sharp departure from the daily demand zone most likely leaves a number of unfilled orders. As a result, the daily demand zone should be the TP for any short trade from the supply zone above. The long tail on candle 1 suggests that some buy orders near the demand zone have been consumed. Similarly, the tails of candles 2 and 3 also suggest the gradual removal of some pending sell orders near the supply zone above. However, these sell orders are not enough to push the price lower than the tail of candle 1, meaning that the buyers are still in control. It is important to remember that a supply zone that has been touched more than once must be treated with caution. This means that the first touch of the zone is not the best entry point.

Candle 4, which is a large body candle showing a sharp movement in price, is created based on the fact that many sell orders have already been consumed by candles 2 and 3. It also created a temporary demand zone (shown by a green rectangle at the base of candle 4 in this Figure 86 (a gray rectangle if you are using the paper edition of this book)) that should be treated as another TP level for my short trade. When I set two TP levels, I can then adjust my supply zone on the 4H chart to plan for a reasonable risk/reward trade.

Let's assume that I place my sell order on the first touch of the daily supply zone on the 4H chart with the risk of the entire zone range. This is illustrated in Figure 87.

Figure 87. Risk/reward ratio based on daily zones marked on the 4H USDJPY chart

You might also agree with me that this kind of ratio, based on the daily chart, is not anywhere close to a reasonable value. It is very important to notice that the presence of the large body candle on the 4H chart (candle 4) is the determining factor for my trade. In fact, without that candle, my TP level could have been the daily demand

131

zone with a distance of almost 215 pips from the touch of the daily supply zone. Such a TP amount would make the choice of the touch of the daily supply zone as the sell entry a reasonable choice, with a risk/reward ratio of 107/215=0.49.

Knowing the first TP level, I should refine the supply zone in order to find a better risk/reward ratio. Hence, the refined supply zone based on the 4H chart was marked with the aid of a gap area as shown in Figure 86. In this kind of scenario, the risk/reward ratio criterion below 0.5 allows me to place my SL well above the supply zone of the daily chart. This is illustrated in Figure 88.

Figure 88. Determining SL and TPs based on the refined SZ

As can be seen on this chart, the refinement of the supply zone based on the 4H chart allows me to extend my risk level to the top border of the daily supply zone. The first TP will provide a sell trade with about a 0.45 ratio, which is reasonable for my trading style. The next TP and ratio calculation is unnecessary at this point. This is due to the fact that if the price moves in my expected direction and reaches TP1, I will move my SL to the breakeven or perhaps into some profit. At this point, my planning for the trade is done and it is very unlikely that I will change my plan even if I learn of a significant upcoming news event. The use of a high time frame such as 4H for my trade execution allows me to avoid the effect of large spreads during such events.

As can be seen in Figure 89, the trades reached the first TP in less than two days. As this point, I had closed half of my sell order and re-evaluated my trade plan. The move downward that is responsible for removing the temporary demand zone near TP1 has now created another temporary supply zone, shown in Figure 89 by the rectangle marked as "New SZ created". My thought is that there has been a considerable number of sell orders in the market that caused the removal of the demand zone. As a result, the probability of some leftover unfilled orders is the highest near that sell area. I do not want to stay in my sell trade if the price is able to remove all of those orders and reach back up the supply zone. This is why I have moved my SL for the second half of the order to above the newly formed supply zone. In fact, I could have added to my short position because the general theme for this currency pair is still bearish, based on the higher time frame analysis.

Figure 89. The sell from the refined SZ reached the first target

Figure 90 shows that the newly formed supply zone indeed had some potential for being used as a measure to decide whether to refine the SL or add to my short position.

Figure 90. The effectiveness of the new SZ for SL modification

Figure 91. The effectiveness of the DZ

Moreover, as you can see in Figure 91, the daily demand zone is still intact and some buy orders still remain to move the price up. This is why you do not want to stay in a sell trade near such a high buying probability region. More importantly, you would not want to be a seller or start a sell position near this kind of demand zone. Regardless of how the price will break or respect this demand zone, you would never enter a sell order near a demand zone.

USDCAD- Feb. 10, 2016

Duration: **medium term** | Time frames: **1D-4H-1H** | Profit/Loss=**245 pips**

Figure 92 shows the daily chart of the USDCAD on Wednesday, February 10th, 2016. The USD had been very strong, reaching an historic 1.45 against the CAD just 20 days beforehand. However, the pair had been showing some weakness in the subsequent two weeks following that high. Although I had been watching the pair for a few days, February 10th was the day that I started my chart analysis. In the previous two days, the pair had shown significant drops during the London sessions. I will provide some more information on these drops on the lower time frame charts.

Figure 92. USDCAD daily chart on Feb. 10, 2016

Q1: Please take a few moments and examine this daily chart. What are the important price levels and what is the overall trend?

Figure 93 shows my analysis of the daily chart with the most important supply and demand zones marked up on the chart. On the daily chart, the pair has broken a major demand zone (seen on the bottom left-hand side of the chart), as well as some other demand zones which can be seen on the 8H or 4H charts (the charts for these time frames are not shown here). I have only marked the most recent supply zone on this chart and it has not been violated by the current price action. Although not marked on this chart, other recent supply zones (only shown by arrows) have also not been violated. The appearance of large bearish candles convinced me that the current sentiment of the market was bearish on this pair.

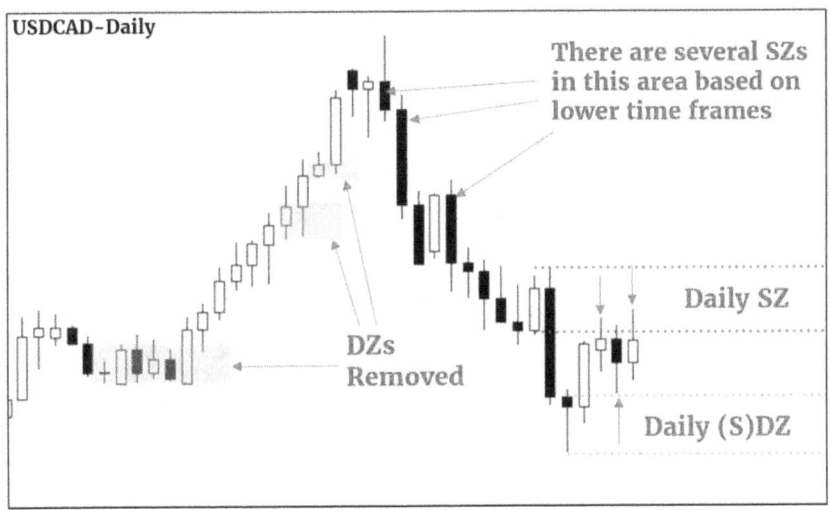

Figure 93. SZs and DZs marked on the USDCAD daily chart (you'll read below that (S)DZ stands for semi-demand zone)

After identifying the most recent zones, you will also notice a few price spikes into the zones. It is important to pay attention to the behavior of each candle, especially those near the zones. At this point, it seems that I am somewhat late in my analysis of the chart, and I have missed the spikes into the supply zone (which were perfect entry points). The current demand zone shown on the chart is not a true demand zone. In this situation, I would rather call it a *semi-demand zone* (abbreviated as (S)DZ in Figures 93 and 94) because it has not broken any major supply zone. However, the strong departure of the price from this zone still makes it significant and worth paying attention to.

Regardless, the trend is still bearish, and finding short entry levels is the most appropriate action. The 4H chart is my medium-term analysis chart to confirm the strength of this bearish trend. However, the distance between the top and the bottom of the current supply and demand zones is somewhat too large for me to be able to make any decision. If I were to use these daily zones, the risk/reward ratio would not yield any reasonable trade. Hence, refining the zones on the 4H chart seems inevitable.

Figure 94. Refining the zones on the 4H chart

As the 4H chart in Figure 94 shows, I modified the range of the supply and semi-demand zones based on this chart. This modification now allows me to look for better entry levels with lower risk. The overall bearish trend also confirms my analysis of the daily chart.

The time frame of execution in this case is the 1H chart. I still believe that I can find a good entry point for a short trade. However, I need to make the decision based on the lower time frame of 1H because I know the price has already twice reacted to the supply zone. If the price leaves the supply zone from the current price, I would rather stay out of any trade because the risk/reward analysis does not fit my criteria.

Figure 95 shows the 1H chart of the USDCAD on February 10th, at around the middle of the US trading session. At this point, judging from the sharp hourly drop candles, my feeling is that I have missed the opportunity to enter the market with my short order. I therefore start looking for a more realistic entry that might allow me to enter the market before it fully drops to the demand zone. The presence of the long tail candles shown by arrows on this chart further supports my short trade idea. These tails are indications of the buy orders being removed along the way. Moreover, any possible temporary demand zone has now been already touched and pending buy orders most likely have been consumed. This is an ideal scenario for an easy drop to the daily demand zone. I decide to place a sell order at the touch of the 1H-SZ that I found based on the Drop-Base-Drop chart pattern.

Figure 95. 1H USDCAD chart used for making the trade decision

Although the range of the hourly supply zone does not extend beyond the 4H-SZ, I decide to place two sell orders near the touch of each zone. Figure 96 shows my risk/reward analysis for each order.

Q2: Can you determine your choice of SL and TP for this trade based on the new 1H-SZ?

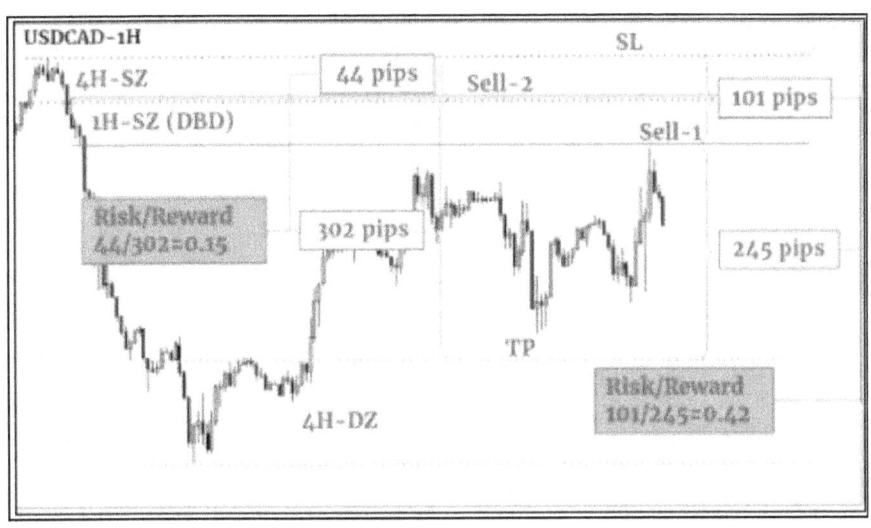

Figure 96. Risk/reward analysis based on two sell orders on a 1H USDCAD chart

As this figure shows, the two sell orders are placed near the touch of the 1H and 4H supply zones. For Sell-1, I am assuming a larger risk/reward ratio compared to Sell-2. However, my anticipation is that it is unlikely to reach the 4H supply zone due to the current price action. At this stage, I only observe the behavior of the market, without making any changes in my plan. In fact, on that very day, I was expecting some volatility during a speech by the Federal Reserve Chair at around 2PM EST. Nevertheless, nothing significant occurred during that time, and I almost lost my hope for being able to execute this trade. However, as mentioned earlier, there was a pattern of significant drops during the London session. I therefore left my trade open overnight in the hope of some volatility that would trigger my order. The outcome of this trade is shown in Figure 97 on the 1H chart.

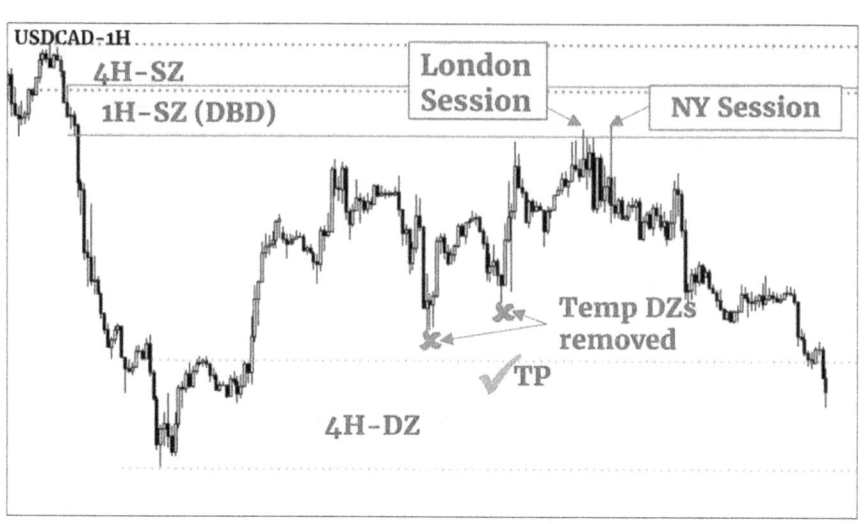

Figure 97. USDCAD short trade results

As this chart suggests, the trade was triggered overnight (my time zone is PST). The price made another attempt to enter into the 1H-SZ during the New York session but failed. Although only one of my sell trades was triggered, I still kept Sell-2 open for another few hours. As I expected, the temporary demand zones were too weak to cause any significant reaction in the price. The trade reached the TP within two days. Now that I look back, the pair did not reach the second order entry even after a time span of almost two years. I hope that this example shows the importance of the multiple time frame analysis and how making a critical decision based on the lowest time frame can result in a profitable trade. As always, thinking about the underlying meaning of candle bars is quite essential for confirming a winning trade. Several techniques and tricks can also be applied to minimize your risk and manage the trade along its course, but they are more advanced and beyond the scope of this book. Adding more complexity to such a simple and yet effective trading strategy is not my intention in writing this book. Let's move on now to the next example.

AUDUSD- Apr. 27, 2016 to June 07, 2016

Duration: 42 days | Time frames: **1D-4H-1H** | Profit/Loss=**582 pips**

The detailed thought process of finding the proper trade setup and conducting multiple time frame analysis was fully explained in the previous examples. In this section, I would like to walk you through the month of May in 2016 where I traded the AUDUSD pair on both the buy and sell side. I will only explain my trade planning based on the daily charts, however, the process of deciding the entry point and fine-tuning the trades also involved the lower time frames of 4H and 1H as seen in the previous examples. My intention is to demonstrate that you do not need to open and close trades every minute or every hour in order to make a good profit. Moreover, it is necessary to understand that trading involves both profit and loss. At the end, it is the sum of the profits and losses that makes the overall performance. It is important to be able to absorb losses when the fundamental driving forces behind a pair change and the trade moves against your prediction. However, one needs patience and perseverance in order to realize whether a move in price is a true change in the overall perspective of the market or if it is just a sudden move by the big players to consume many of the SL orders from retail traders. (Please see Chapter 2, where I talk about a "smart" mechanism hidden behind the scenes that is shopping for your SL.)

Figure 98 shows the overall picture of the AUDUSD pair on the 1D chart as at April 27th, 2016. As can be seen, I have indicated four major zones that, in my opinion, can be traded. The type of each zone is also indicated by the acronyms on the chart. The first and nearest zone is the supply zone that has broken some recent demand zones to its left, as shown by the arrow. It should be noted that the demand zone shown by the arrow does not have significant quality. However, it is a zone that the price had moved away from in an upward direction and, hence, its breaking indicates some strength in the now downward price movement.

Figure 98. AUDUSD daily chart with SZs and DZs marked

In the following figures, I will reference only the nearest zone to avoid overcrowding the charts with multiple zones. Looking at the current price, the currency pair seems to be responding to a demand zone that is a Rally-Base-Rally. However, I have not entered any long trades since I was not paying attention to this particular zone at the time. Figure 99 shows the response to this Rally-Base-Rally zone in the following days. My trade, as indicated on the chart, is a sell order at the bottom of the supply zone.

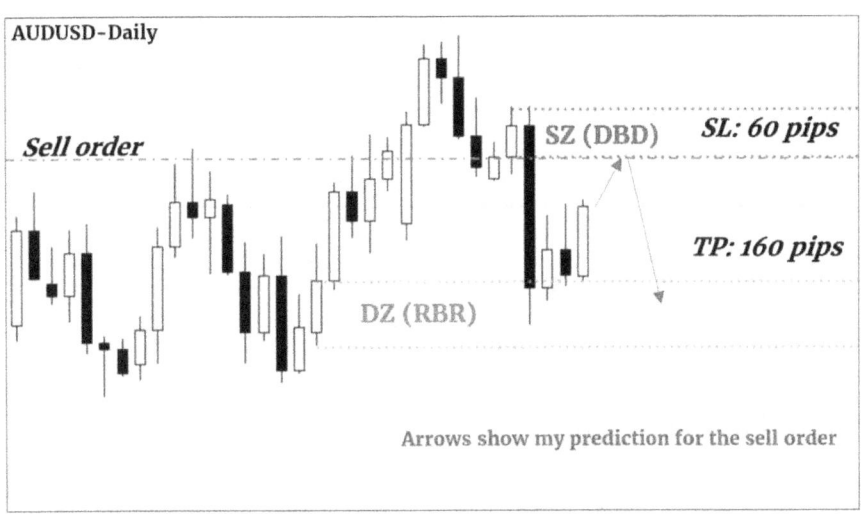

Figure 99. AUDUSD daily chart with sell order based on the SZ

The SL and TP levels are also indicated on this chart. Please keep in mind that I am monitoring the trade and price action using the lower 4H and 1H time frames. The current TP is based on the nearest demand zone, which is still not broken, and hence is a good area to take profit.

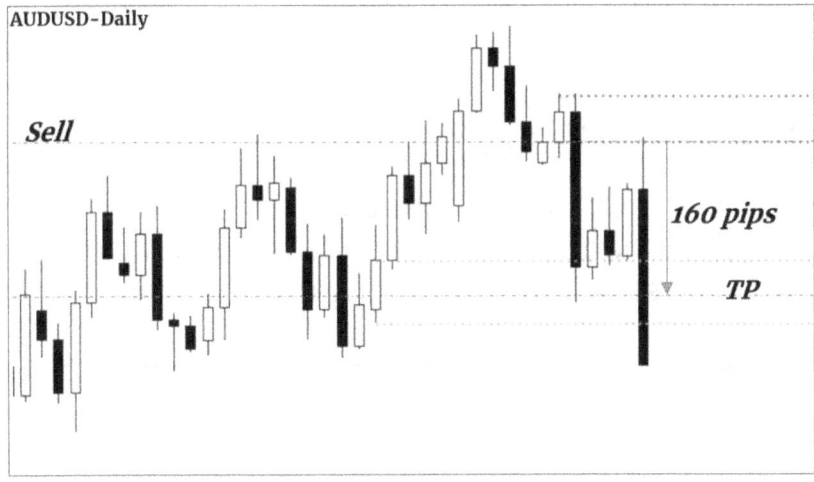

Figure 100. Daily and 1H charts of the AUDUSD after the triggering of the sell order

As Figure 100 shows, the sell order was triggered once the price reached to its level, which was then followed by a sharp drop. The reason behind the drop was the Reserve Bank of Australia's (RBA) unexpected decrease in their interest rate to 1.75% versus the 2.00% expected forecast. As the hourly chart shows, the drop consisted of a sharp drop toward my original TP level followed by a retracement and further drop that broke the Rally-Base-Rally demand zone. At this point, I became more confident in the starting of a new downtrend based both on the interest rate decision and the price action showing strong downward pressure. The structure of the daily chart at this stage does not provide any good sell entry point. However, there exists two demand zones on the way down that I will utilize for some short-term long trades. This is shown in Figure 101 where I placed a buy order near the demand zone.

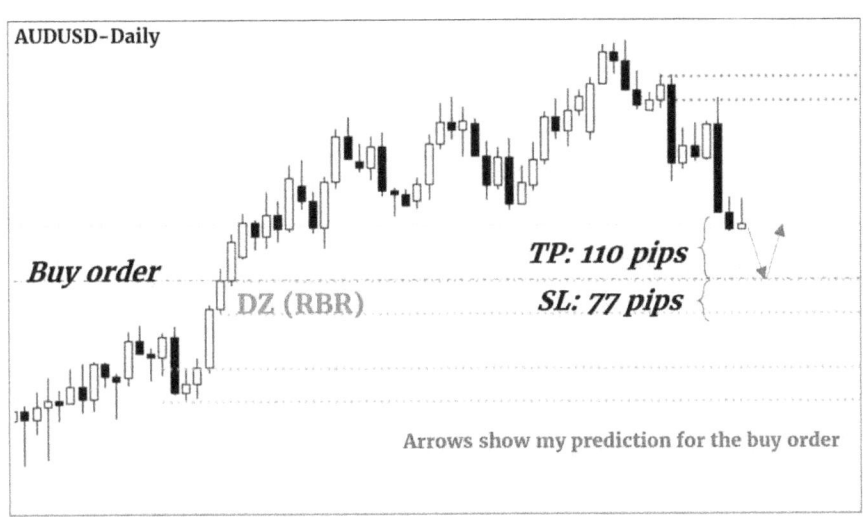

Figure 101. Buy order for the AUDUSD based on the DZ

As can be seen by the TP and SL amounts, this buy order has a high risk/reward ratio that in the ideal situation should not have been taken. However, this is what occurred in my trade planning in real time and represents a good lesson to learn. Figure 102 shows what happened in the following days.

As the chart in Figure 102 shows, the price moved further down into the demand zone and then moved back up from that zone. At this point, I was still expecting the price to reach my TP level which was near a supply zone that was of a Drop-Base-Drop type. However, to reduce my risk further, I moved my SL a few pips up toward the recent low as indicated on the chart. In this scenario, I was risking 40 pips to achieve the original 110 pips at the TP.

Figure 102. Daily AUDUSD chart after the buy order

Figure 103 shows what happened in the following days after I modified my original trade plan. As can be seen, the price moved further down without reaching the TP level and my SL was reached. A total of 40 pips was lost on this trade. However, as shown on this chart, a new supply zone was created due to the break of the demand zone. Hence, I placed a new sell order near the bottom of this new supply zone, aiming for the next demand zone.

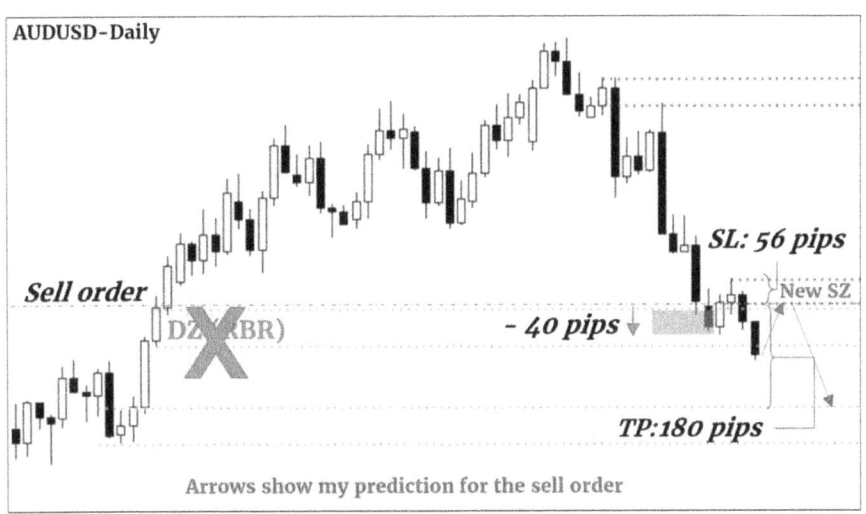

Arrows show my prediction for the sell order

Figure 103. AUDUSD 1D chart, SL reached in buy order, new sell order placed

The sell order has about a 0.3 risk/reward ratio (56/180=0.3), which makes it a very reasonable choice for a trade. It should be clear at this point that the recently created supply zone is of a Drop-Base-Drop type and the currency pair is still clearly in a downtrend. Taking trades against the dominant trend is always riskier and should be carefully monitored to minimize the risk. However, one could argue that it is always better to stay with the trend and avoid trading such scenarios. In my opinion, it is a personal choice which must be taken, considering your risk appetite and the size of your account. I often take high risk/reward ratio trades because they offer tremendous profits at the end. In other words, I am willing to sacrifice calculated amounts of risk in return for catching a reversal in a trend. Let's continue and see the progress of the trade on this pair, as set out in Figure 104.

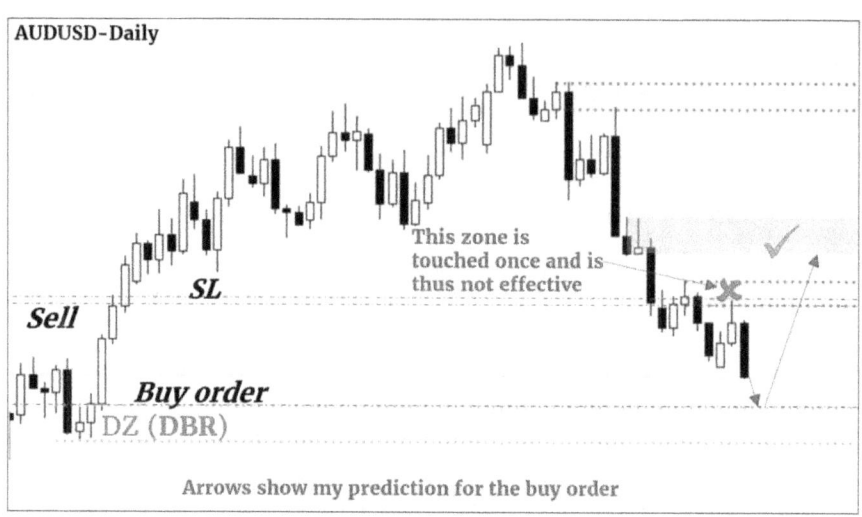

Figure 104. Sell entry triggered and new buy order placed on 1D AUDUSD

The sell entry was triggered, and the price moved down sharply from that level. At this point, you can see that I have already moved my SL further down near the breakeven to minimize the risk. I have also placed another buy order near the top of the demand zone, which has not been touched since early March. The SL for this buy order is below the bottom of the zone and the TP level is near a recent supply zone that has not been touched, as indicated on the right-hand side of the chart by the shaded rectangular box and the check mark. The rationale behind selecting such a distant TP level is based on the price action having already reached the demand zone. The nearest supply zone that has had significance is the zone where I entered the sell trade. However, as the cross sign indicates, this zone has been touched once in the past, and I do not anticipate many unfilled orders left near that zone. The next big bearish candle that is currently where the price is at has not yet broken the demand zone and I do not consider it to be important. Again, the price action when approaching the demand zone determines whether or not I keep this buy order on my chart.

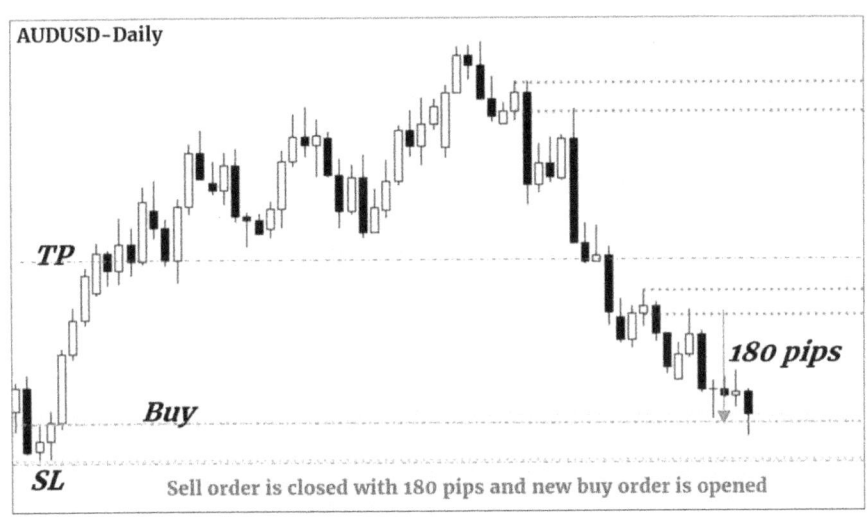

Figure 105. I exit the sell and enter the buy trade, as marked on the 1D AUDUSD chart

As this chart in Figure 105 shows, the sell TP was reached five days after I entered the trade. The reason I mention the duration is to emphasize the importance of patience and execution based on your original plan. At the same time, my buy entry was triggered and I was in the long trade with the anticipation of a major trend reversal. As you can see, my TP level was near the supply zone where I predicted that some unfilled sell orders still existed. The reason that I was not considering the most recent supply zone is that it had not broken any major demand zone at the time. It had also been touched once, making it somewhat weak as a supply zone.

Figure 106 shows the price movement after the buy entry and how it reacted to the nearest supply zone. The price stalled at that zone for a day and then broke above the zone the next day. It took about 10 days from my buy entry for the price to reach the TP level.

Figure 106. I exit the buy order at the TP level, 1D AUDUSD chart

This is a total of four trades that I took over the course of 42 days (the last few days of April, the entire month of May, and the first few days of June 2016). I did not track the trades following the last trade outlined here. However, the reasoning and analysis remains similar to what I explained in this section. Figure 107 shows a picture of the pair in early July 2016, a month after my last recorded trade. I have marked two new zones and removed other zones based on the price action. I used these new zones in my trading for this pair during that month.

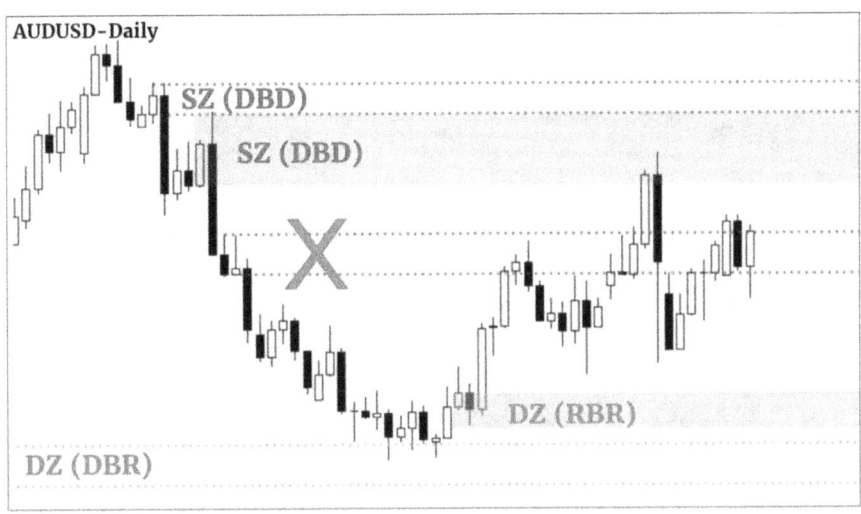

Figure 107. The AUDUSD daily chart during the month following the last trade

It would be useful for you to take a look at this chart and mark various zones you observe and make some plans for trades that you would have taken if you were looking at this chart in real time. For instance, the new supply zone shown by the shaded box marked "SZ (DBD)" would have resulted in a very profitable sell trade.

In this next section, I will dive deeper into the details of the four trades detailed above that I took in the AUDUSD pair. I will explain how the real account that I used grew during this 42-day long test. I will also demonstrate a few key parameters that are always involved in any forex trading and must be continually taken into account.

Figure 108 summarizes the results of these trades in the AUDUSD pair during the aforementioned period. The box at the top of the plots shows the account information used for this test.

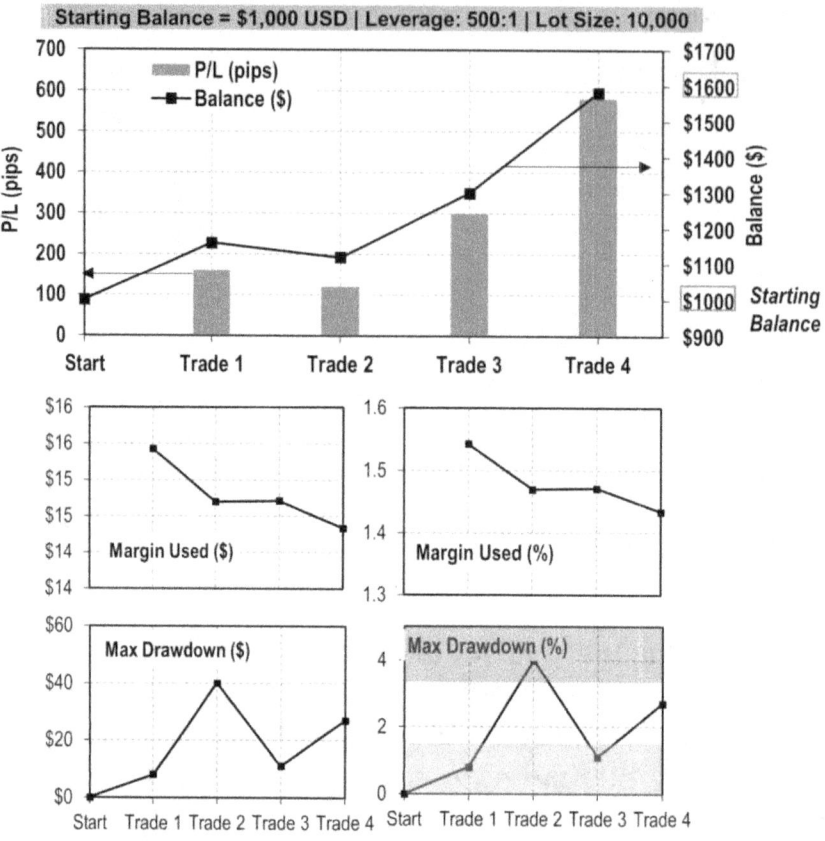

Figure 108. Summary of my four trades in AUDUSD during 42 days in 2016. Note: in the top graph, the left axis represents the pip values shown by the bar chart and the right axis represents the account balance shown by the line chart.

The real account that I used in this example was highly leveraged (500:1) and had a starting balance of $1,000 USD. Please note that the use of high leverage is accompanied by an equally high level of risk. For many starter accounts, a leverage of 50:1 or 30:1 is recommended. Using a large leverage allows me to implement a simple rule I almost always use when selecting the appropriate lot size. You may recall that earlier in this book I mentioned that forex pairs have historically been traded only in specific amounts called lots, which are the number of currency pair units being traded. The standard lot size is 100,000 units of a currency pair. Accordingly, in most cases, the number of standard lots (100,000) I select for trading is a multiple of 10 times the total balance in my account. The table below, marked as Figure 109, shows an example of this principle. To walk you through the first line in this table, if I have $500 in my account, $500 x 10 = 5,000, and 5,000 is 0.05 of a standard lot of 100,000 units.

Balance	Lot Size (Standard Lot)
$500	0.05
$1,000	0.1
$5,000	0.5

Figure 109. Choosing the size of lot appropriate for the account size

Drawdown - how much to risk?

It should be noted that your choice of lot size is strongly dependent on your amount of leverage as well as your account balance. In some cases where multiple trades are active on different pairs at the same time, the required margin for your account could make it difficult to absorb the necessary amount of risk, referred to as the drawdown, in each trade. The drawdown is the amount of lost capital compared to the maximum capital in your account. Here, I refer to the drawdown as the maximum loss that I am willing to absorb in each trade before reaching my TP. When several trades are open during a given period, the drawdown in some trades could exceed the amount of your eligible margin. Therefore, it is possible that the platform, or your broker to be more precise, will automatically close those trades. An example of this kind of scenario is when you have set the SL at a specific level and yet your broker closes your trade prior to reaching that SL. The trade that could have been a winning one would thus be prematurely closed due to an insufficient margin in your account. The insufficient margin is not necessarily due to the large amount of risk you are taking, but could also arise from having multiple trades open at the same time.

In order to avoid scenarios like this, which happen quite often, the use of a larger account balance or higher leverage is beneficial. A popular rule among traders is not to risk more than 2% of your total balance in any trade. This means for a $1,000 account, a total risk of $20 in each trade. In some of my trades, I consider risk values of up to 4% of my total balance. After all, many factors are involved in considering the amount of risk for a trade. These include the entry level, the size of the zone, and the timing of economic news releases about a company.

Let's go back to the example now and walk through the charts shown in Figure 108. Since my account balance starts at $1,000 USD, $1,000 x 10 = 10,000, and 10,000 is 0.1 of a standard lot of 100,000 units. This is constant throughout all of these trades. The top chart combines the total number of pips made after each trade, as shown on the left axis. The right axis shows the equivalent dollar amount that is added to the initial balance of $1,000 USD. As can be seen, over the period of 42 days, the four trades have resulted in the total amount of about 600 pips, which translates to $600 USD in profit. This corresponds to a 60% growth in the size of the account during this period.

The plots at the bottom left show the actual dollar value of the margin and drawdown incurred in each trade. Due to the high leverage amount, an average amount of $14-$15 USD was used for each trade. Similarly, the dollar amount of the drawdown varies between $10-$40 USD for these trades. The highest drawdown occurred when the SL was reached in the 2nd trade. Converting these values to the percentage of the total balance indicates, in my opinion, an aggressive trading style. While I am using 1-1.5% of my capital for each trade, I am risking up to 4% of my capital, a slightly aggressive strategy. As I indicated, a risk of below 2% of the total balance of your account is a reasonable amount for considering in each trade. Taking risk over 4% is not recommended because it could gradually result in severe losses over the long term.

In general, this type of analysis should always be done as a routine process during your trading. Understanding how much you risk and what to expect from your broker's platform in the case of overtrading is important in order to achieve a sustainable forex trading strategy. This example was recorded mainly for the purpose of demonstrating the potential of supply and demand trading as a swing style strategy. As you can see, the total number of four trades in 42 days translates into an average of one trade per 10 days. It is extremely important to understand that remaining patient and not taking every trade that you see in the news outlets you are following does not mean that you are losing out. In fact, by not taking many of the trades recommended by these news outlets, you are actually doing your account a favor. You do not need to open five or ten trades a day in order to be a successful forex trader. However, you can always choose to become a day trader in forex using the lower time frame charts. Being aware of the total number of pips made each day is very critical. In the end, achieving a total number of almost 600 pips in 42 days on a single pair using a swing or day trading strategy is considered to be a successful strategy. The difference is your preference for staring at charts for extended periods of time during the day or tracking a trade once or twice each day.

CHAPTER 4: CONCLUDING REMARKS

This book summarizes the basic principles that I have learned through my past almost 10 years of practice in forex trading. Throughout this book, basic concepts such as the terminology of forex trading, opening an account and chart analysis, as well as two effective strategies, were explained. These are the very same concepts and strategies I use in my own daily trading process.

The most important message I would like you to take away from this book is that trading takes practice. You should not expect to be able to immediately implement the concepts that were explained in this book in your own trading. The road to becoming a consistent winner is long and requires a deep understanding of both your inner psychological behavior and market behavior.

This might sound familiar to you if you have ever traded any instrument like stocks, options or a forex pair. By starting the journey of trading, you learn many new facts about your own behavior, your responses to basic instincts such as fear and greed, and your opinions about the role that economics plays in our daily lives. Moreover, you must and will find out how the immense number of market players, including retail traders and big bank traders, behave at any given time in terms of making contradictory decisions. In my experience, one must be a market player in order to understand the behavior of its participants. Studying textbooks and taking online training are only beneficial if you decide to "get your hands dirty in the field". Like many things in life, you will learn more by making mistakes. When you start trading, you will no doubt end up on the wrong side of some trades and that is when your brain will best be able to rationalize and process your decision-making. Within the framework of trading, making mistakes is equal to losing your money. You need to minimize this loss by practicing risk management. Throughout this book, either when explaining the strategies or during the real-life examples, I have brought up this key concept in different contexts.

Another important concept is the value of understanding the price action through analyzing price charts. The charts contain all of the information you need to know in order to make your trading decisions. It is only a matter of training your eyes and mindset when observing the charts. Through some practical examples, I have explained a different way of looking at a chart in order to understand the behavior of the market players. Please keep in mind that a simple change in the appearance of a chart does not resolve the underlying story behind the chart. It only provides a new window through which you can gain new insights from price behavior. Nevertheless, you can use practice methods similar to what I have shown in this book to train your eyes to understand charts. Do not expect to understand the reason behind every single candle you see on your chart because it is not necessary. You only need to get enough information to find the level or region that is of interest to the big market players. Make the effort of distinguishing the significant levels from the noise of the market, which is mostly caused by individual brokers.

As an important factor in determining your trading style, multiple time frame analysis can have both negative and positive impacts on your trading results. Analyzing your charts using an excessive number of time frames can be misleading. Depending on your trading style and availability to look at charts throughout the day, choosing a sequence of time frames appropriate for your trading style is essential. Although the trading strategies outlined in this book are valid for any sequence of time frames, my personal preference is the sequence of three time frames consisting of daily, 4H and 1H charts. In my experience, three time frames should provide you with enough information to make a trade decision. While the higher time frame usually provides hints about the overall direction of the market, lower time frames are tools for fine-tuning the entry and exit levels. In any case, the choice of your entry and exit as well as risk should be estimated using a single set of time frames. In most cases, the higher time frames supersede the lower time frames in terms of importance and strength. This concept has been explained throughout the book using chart demonstrations and real-life examples.

Consider this book and its content as an opening door to the big world of institutional traders. While we as individual retail traders do not have access to the vast sea of knowledge that they have, we should still be looking for their footprints on the charts as well as in other online resources. The chart tells the whole story. However, there are more advanced tools and data analysis methods that can help decipher the story easier. Looking at the number of trades institutional traders have placed each week and realizing their overall mindset is something that can be done. The data is available to the public, but it is time-consuming and tiring to analyze. Bringing those rigorous data analysis methodologies into the content of this book defeats the purpose of this book: to introduce you to the world of big forex traders. I will leave it to you to decide to dig deeper into the numbers. I assure you that I will be there to help if you make that decision.

Last but not least, if you found the material in this book useful, I would appreciate your taking a few minutes to provide a review on the Amazon website. Receiving honest feedback from your reviews is key to the success of this book. I will certainly consider your comments in making revisions. Your review on Amazon will help others make informed decisions when deciding to purchase my book. The price is set low to ensure the book is affordable for everyone and thus I can share what I have learned about forex trading with the widest possible audience. Helping others start a new journey and career path is what brings me fulfillment and teaches me new lessons every day. For me, there is always room to learn more. I hope you can help me accomplish this goal of mine.